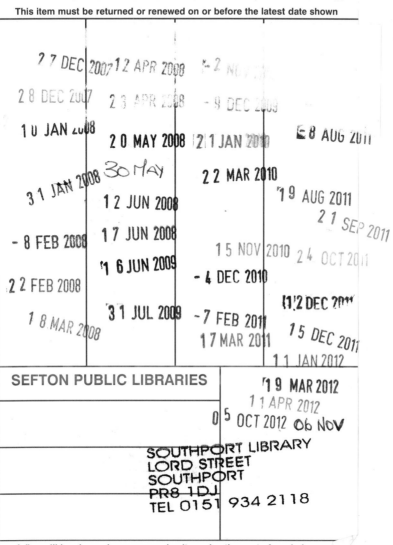

SOUTHPORT

STORIES AND LANDSCAPES

SOUTHPORT
STORIES AND LANDSCAPES

DAVID LEWIS

breedon **books**
PUBLISHING

First published in Great Britain in 2005 by

The Breedon Books Publishing Company Limited

Breedon House, 3 The Parker Centre, Derby, DE21 4SZ.

ISBN 1 85983 467 1

Printed and bound by Biddles Ltd, King's Lynn, Suffolk.

CONTENTS

DEDICATION

To my late aunt,

Margaret Gwynneth Jones.

She was full of travellers' tales and

taught me the importance of the

smallest stories.

ACKNOWLEDGEMENTS

Many people came up with stories and ideas to follow for a book on Southport's landscapes, but in no particular order I would especially like to thank the following people for their assistance in writing this book: Susan Last and the staff of Breedon Books, who took the initial idea on board straight away; Jo Jones and Philip Rowe at Sefton Arts, who were most helpful with contacts and suggestions; Lindsey McCormick at the Botanic Gardens Museum, who gave me her valuable time to rummage through the archives and who was also very generous in making images electronically accessible. Andrew Farthing and the local studies team at the central library found many interesting pictures and maps of old Southport and gave invaluable advice on what could be realistically used, and I am grateful for the many hours they spent scanning images and sending them to me. My parents Dorothy and Reg Lewis were supportive and curious over tea and crosswords, and my good friend Jeff Young gave good advice on style and presentation; and finally I couldn't write anything without the love and enthusiastic support of my partner, Justine Cook.

Picture credits:
All archive images reproduced by kind permission of Sefton MBC Leisure Services Department, Arts and Cultural Services, Botanic Gardens Museum.

FURTHER READING

Hopefully the stories and especially the dates in this book are supported by historical or architectural fact. I found Peter Aughton's book, *North Meols and Southport – A History*, a rich source of story and atmosphere. *Southport – A Pictorial History* by Harry Foster is well illustrated and very well written, as is his history of Birkdale. Sylvia Harrop's book, *Families and Cottages of Old Birkdale and Ainsdale*, brought a lost, older landscape to life. *Murray's Lancashire Architectural Guide* by Peter Fleetwood-Hesketh is a monumental book on the buildings of Lancashire which helped me see Southport in a new light, as did Cedric Greenwood's excellent *Thatch, Towers and Colonnades*, which has been reprinted recently. *Annals of Southport and District – A Chronological History of North Meols from Alfred the Great to Edward the Seventh* by E. Bland had some fascinating and also some dubious history in it, as well as stories from Charles Legh's book, *History of Lancashire, Cheshire and Derbyshire*, which was originally published in 1700. Books of old photographs of the town I found extremely useful, especially Ian Simpson's book on Southport for the 'Images of England' series and *Southport As It Was* by Joan Tarbuck, published in 1972. F.W. Robinson's *Descriptive History of Southport* from 1848 was reprinted for the town's bicentenary in 1992 and had some interesting stories and patronising opinions. *Southport a Century Ago* by Geoff Wright, also published for the bicentenary, had a reprint of an excellent travellers' guide to the town first published in 1889, which made for laborious but fascinating reading. William Ashton's 1909 book, *The Battle of Land and Sea*, and the more modern *The Sands of Time* by Philip Smith taught me much about the coastline. *Sun, Sand and Silver Wings* by John Mulliner is the story of aviation in Southport told lightly and with faint nostalgia. Rob Gell's *An Illustrated Survey of Railway Stations between Southport and Liverpool 1848–1986* has inspired me to explore old railway lines for many years, and goes into great detail about Southport's lost stations. Finally, Charles Nevin's book

Lancashire, Where Women Die of Love is a rollercoaster ride through places and people, dragging true stories along behind it. After completing this book, *Martin Mere, Lancashire's Lost Lake* was published. Written by W.G. Hale and Audrey Coney, this is the book I wanted to read during my research, but it came out too late to be of any use to me.

I also found the Internet useful in tracking ideas and nailing down facts. Online research threw up lots of stories, from how to get into lost underground Nevill Street to the memories of bomber crews recuperating in the Palace Hotel. I found these websites especially useful: mersey-gateway.com is a general Merseyside website, but has some good Southport articles on it as does virtualsouthport.co.uk; seftoncoast.org.uk and sefton.gov.uk are generally useful local sites. I found more stories on knowhere.co.uk with its lists of local heroes, and mightyseas.co.uk, where the account of the coroner's court for the *Mexico* disaster was brought to life. thrustssc.com has the story of the 'Southport Sunbeams', the giant cars which once ran for the land speed record on the sands here, stories I still find difficult to believe. My personal favourite site was southport.gb.com, with its mixture of local news and sport, business advertising and events. Chasing the threads in the 'past' section was especially rewarding. There are informative and nostalgic articles posted here, including John Ashton's essay on the Altcar Bob railway line, as well as more everyday memories of old shops, bus routes, clubs, restaurants and railway stations. I never did rediscover the website of Birkdale holiday memories.

CHAPTER ONE

A LANDSCAPE OF FENS AND BIRDS

Southport is a town surrounded by water, or the memory of water. Four hundred years ago the rich agricultural landscape inland of the town was a marshy patchwork of small lakes or meres and patches of low-lying boggy ground which were called mosses, with small islands of higher ground between them. The islands divided the landscape and allowed each marsh to be named, and some of these names have survived: Churchtown Moss, Birkdale Moss, Blowick Moss. This patchwork stretched from Tarleton to Altcar or even Crosby, and perhaps at the northern end it merged imperceptibly with the salt marshes and low islands of Churchtown and Marshside, threatened from the west by salt tides and surrounded by fens. This landscape ran for many miles away from the sea, and even today the maps for Mawdesley and Croston are still criss-crossed by drainage ditches. Only here does the land begin to rise.

This flat landscape exposed to the sea weather must have been a bleak place to live, and it is perhaps small wonder that it was only thinly populated for many centuries. But this land has always been crossed by people. There were settlements on the islands and perhaps fishermen and farmers from the scattered coastal villages of North Meols, Formby or Ainsdale came warily onto the mosses for fish and game, and to hunt the great flocks of wintering birds; perhaps there were also wooden stilt-roads across the shallower marshes to allow hunters to reach the birds, which grew into small routes across the fenland. East from Birkdale or Ainsdale tracks guided travellers to mediaeval villages and churches such as Halsall, built on the low islands of solid ground. There were routes from Birkdale to Scarisbrick and on to the important churches at Ormskirk and Burscough Priory. I am intrigued by these old Catholic pilgrim trails, like Churchgate nearer the sand hills, and it would make sense to me if a northern route across the marshes also guided pilgrims to St Cuthbert's church near the coast. In some cases these church trails were marked by large stone crosses and one of these survives, tucked into the estate wall near the canal at Scarisbrick.

On the Blaeu map of 1662, a copy of which is in Southport Library, the smaller mosses are shaded as one huge area called simply 'Mosse', a name still used by local people for the fields and farms inland from the coastal settlements. On the map this marshy landscape lies between the high sand hills of the coast and the vast fen of Martin Mere, stretching inland towards Rufford and Scarisbrick Hall. I knew of Martin Mere only as the famous bird sanctuary near Ormskirk and had no idea that it was the most famous of the great Lancashire meres. At one time it was seen as the largest lake in England, with a diameter of two miles and a circumference of 18 miles. There are intriguing local connections with the myth of King Arthur and the Knights of the Round Table; Martin Mere is supposedly the place where Arthur was given Excalibur by the Lady of the Lake, and Lancelot's connections with it gave him the surname 'du Lac'. At the end of the legends, the Mere is the water into which Bedivere eventually hurls the great sword, on the wishes of the dying Arthur. Many parts of the country have connections with semi-mythical figures like King Arthur or Robin Hood, examples of myths or storytelling rooted in real landscapes. The Arthur connection with Martin Mere is mentioned but dismissed by many writers, but it must have been rooted here for some reason and at the very least it gives some idea of the prominence of Martin Mere through the ages.

The draining of Martin Mere and the mosses deserves a book to itself, covering the history and dates of ditches, and the characters and stories involved. The work began in 1692, a century before the founding of Southport. Thomas Fleetwood worked with the Hesketh and Scarisbrick estates and other local landowners to dry out the Mere for cultivation. He began by digging a great canal from the coastline near Crossens to the lowest parts of the Mere, and erecting a pair of floodgates near the sea. Fleetwood's Sluice is still there, now one of three large waterways draining the Mere. It runs in a slash across the fields from the pumping station at Crossens to Wiggins Lane at Holmswood, where it joins Boat House Sluice and drains land around the bird sanctuary of modern Martin Mere. By July 1696 a three-mile racecourse had been laid out 'on a parcel of ground called Merton Meare, near Ormskirk' and Fleetwood gave racing prizes to the value of £36, perhaps to demonstrate his confidence in the safety of the reclaimed land. There must have been people who argued that the Mere would

Original paving setts, Red Lion Bridge.

Looking towards Halsall Church from St Aidan's Church, November 2004.

The 'Altcar Bob' trackbed looking towards Southport from Heathey Lane.

New Cut Lane Bridge.

Black Moss, near Scarisbrick Hall.

Boundary Brook drainage ditch, Birkdale Moss.

Scarisbrick wayside cross, hidden in the trees on the busy road to Ormskirk.

A wintry view of Black Moss near Jacksmere Lane.

never be drained, that the work was a fool's errand. But Fleetwood was proved right and over the following 60 or 80 years Martin Mere was drained for cultivation, although maps from the mid-18th century still mark the Mere as being fully dry only in the summer. Thomas Fleetwood never saw the work completed, as he died in 1717. On his memorial in St Cuthbert's in Churchtown the heads of cherubs rise from stone waves, perhaps suggesting hopefully the new lands being freed from the water.

As the land was drained, vast quantities of fish were stranded: roach, eels, pike, perch and bream, which must have been a bonanza for the diggers and local people. No fewer than eight wooden canoes were discovered in the ooze at the bottom of the Mere, some of great

Tarleton Runner.

Thomas Fleetwood's sluice.

age. The canoes seem to have disappeared, but one was eventually rescued by the Reverend Bulpit, a local writer and antiquarian, and is now in the Churchtown museum. The late 17th-century writer Charles Legh mentions the fact that remains of a great 'stag of Canada' were found; 'the brow antlers were bigger than usually the arms of a man is, the beams were near two yards in height and betwixt the two opposite tips of the horns was two yards likewise.' How big must this animal have been, to have had a set of horns six feet from tip to tip? These giant horns were cut up for souvenirs by the locals, and perhaps there are fragments of elk horn in the attics of Halsall and Burscough to this day. Legh also casually mentions how 'sometimes in mosses are found human bodies entire and uncorrupted as in a moss near the meales in Lancashire'. The 'meales' or meols are the sand hills, so perhaps this 'entire and uncorrupted' body was discovered in the draining of the moss at Birkdale or Blowick. Where is it now? Legh's notes conjure up a prehistoric time of people in wooden canoes hunting giant elk, and perhaps reverentially burying their dead in the marshy ground.

The old lake beds were divided up into fields. Not much has been written about how the land was allocated; who did it belong to? Perhaps the meres and mosses had clear legal owners and there were no ownership disputes, but over 3,000 acres of farmland were gained by the draining of Martin Mere alone. The new land was used for growing vegetables as it was generally too good to waste on pasturing animals. The soil is still very rich, and is noticeably darker than the sandy ground of Southport; centuries of peaty decay have made the old marsh beds very fertile. In the autumn great gangs of farm workers still descend on the fields to harvest leeks, sprouts and carrots. It is a strangely mediaeval sight, lines of people doing this backbreaking work in the cold wind. Scoured by fierce winds this can be a very bleak landscape, and the farm buildings are protected from the weather by large hedges and stands of trees. The valuable land is intensively farmed, and there is very little 'wild' countryside apart from a large number of coverts of woodland left to protect the game birds, and the reeds and tall grasses which grow in the ditches. These break the skyline up, and the views across the flat fields are defined by abrupt stands of trees, thick spinneys and bulrushes. But the fact that it is so industrially farmed means that although there are numerous footpaths and bridleways, it is not generally a landscape for recreation.

Sad to say, the best way to see this landscape is as a passenger in a car, which allows time to observe the fields and place-names without being distracted by having to drive. Some of the roads are very busy, as the villages are inhabited by commuters and home-workers as well as farm labourers. The land is crossed by a series of main roads, connecting Southport with Tarleton and Preston, and southwards through Scarisbrick to Ormskirk and Maghull. But many smaller roads run quietly from these busy routes, still called by their old names and too small even to be B-roads. These long, often very straight lanes lead past modern bungalows and isolated houses to the farms on the old mosses. Beyond the farms they join a network of narrow, dusty farm tracks, full of pot holes and gravel, used by tractors and large farm lorries to reach the fields. Driving them in an ordinary car can be a hair-raising experience. The old one-way roads and causeways are raised above the fields, above the watery line of the marsh, and there is very little room to turn around; but these causeways are a physical memory of the fens.

The fields are contained by mile after mile of drainage ditch, and there are pumping stations and even old windmills dotted across the landscape. I walked across the rich fields of Martin Mere on a bright, cold day, the sky high and blue and flecked with wispy cloud. The landscape around me was immense; I could see no other people, just a dog jumping and barking in the farm a big field away, an open-sided lorry with its canvas sides flapping in the wind, a tractor pulling a trailer of potatoes stirring up a dust storm. The ground was dark and dry after a few spring days without rain, but the drainpipes in the ditch to my right were dripping a trickle of water to the sluggish stream at the bottom, some eight or nine feet below me. The sides of the ditch were lined with grasses, cow parsley and dandelions, and buzzed with bees. This field was marked on the map as part of Martin Mere itself. Perhaps this was where Charles Legh's giant elk was found, or one of the wooden canoes, perhaps where Arthur received Excalibur from the Lady of the Lake. A landscape of history and myth. Ahead of me was the line of trees marking Thomas Fleetwood's great Sluice, although – as all the fields are bordered by ditches – I had to find a bridge. The Sluice is a wide channel of brown water: grassy and lined with trees, like an obscure French canal. I found it strange to think that it was first dug in the 1690s and is still draining the old Mere today. Other channels run through this lush, green country; Tarleton Runner, Middle Ditch, smaller waterways fed in turn by the grid pattern of smaller ditches draining every field. It doesn't feel English, this part of western Lancashire. With its straight roads and greenhouses it feels Dutch, with its canals and trees it seems somehow French. It is strange how one place can remind us of somewhere else. Although I am used to this with buildings (especially in Southport) I found it an unusual experience to be reminded of Holland on an English lane; and yet I suppose that this is essentially an inland 'polder', land first reclaimed from the North Sea by the Dutch, and so the model for reclaimed land all over Europe.

In the spring sunshine Martin Mere is a pleasant, lush place, but walking this landscape can be a bleak experience. Once I walked from Southport through Birkdale and out to Scarisbrick, to see the remains of dismantled railway architecture and the Leeds–Liverpool Canal, as the canal boats used to unload Southport visitors at Scarisbrick before the railways arrived in the late 1840s. It was a misty autumn day, damp and bitterly cold. From Birkdale I walked along Moss Road. In the summer the chestnut trees arch over the road and the verges are full of cow parsley, but in November it is a dreary thoroughfare, rural suburbia swamping old farms. But already I was in the parish of Halsall, and I was delighted to see a kingfisher in Fine Jane's Brook. This was clear but lined with weeds and dead grasses, signs of past and future spates; there was a wren in the grasses and mallards further downstream. Moss Road led to a long stumbling walk along a road with no pavements, the verges rocky and overgrown with rock-hard grasses, scattered with rusting litter which was slowly fading into the grass; the whole spattered and drenched with rain, salt-spray, dust, car fumes. The road is raised slightly above the sheep fields and is perhaps the old Birkdale Cop, originally built centuries ago to connect the town with Scarisbrick. There were high thorn bushes to protect grazing animals from wind and rain, and wild teasels, their dry seed heads rattling in the wind. This was once fens and lake-beds, and already the fields on either side of the road were defined by drainage ditches, the dull water glinting in the thin autumnal light. A squat, noisy pumping station stands on the arrow-straight Boundary Brook, desolate and lonely, less than a mile from Moss Road. On foot I realised how rich this landscape is in birds. I had thought of these fields as flat and open, but there are wind break hedges, coverts and stands of trees for protection, as well as the many miles of ditches and streams. There were mallard and other ducks along the ditches, partridges, lapwings and pheasants on the fields, and unseen birds whistling in the thin trees. The large fields opened up the landscape and the distant church at Halsall appeared on the horizon.

The road rears up at the grass business of Turfland and goes over a bridge, one of the railway bridges that dot this landscape like Roman ruins, visible for miles across the fields. From 20 feet up, the horizon towards northern Southport was dominated by the grey and white gasometer, standing tall like a colour chart for the sky. There was a line of new houses and a smudge of trees, telegraph lines and fields of sheep. Towards the coast were the low roofs of Moss Road and the trees and occasional towers of Birkdale. This bridge once ran over Heathey Lane Halt, a small railway station on the famous Altcar Bob line from Southport to Downholland. A scramble down muddy paths led to the old trackbed, running dead straight towards Kew Gardens in Southport, a giant rusty farm machine crouched in the old bridge space like a tethered elephant. The stonework is still crisp, although folding back into the landscape and overgrown with brambles. After closure in the 1930s, Heathey Lane was used for storing old rolling stock and the last train ran here in the early 1960s, but the stone arch beneath the road was still crusted with soot or 'blackened from its gasping', in John Ashcroft's poetic phrase. His account of the Altcar Bob line, available online, roots it firmly in this landscape and the stories and memories of the people who lived here. The railway company built smaller bridges and drainage ditches as defences against the rising water;

A spring day in Pinfold,
Scarisbrick, looking towards
Red Lion Bridge.

it must have been an engineering feat to build a railway line across the moss, the Victorian engineers surely benefiting from George Stephenson's achievement in taking the Liverpool–Manchester line across Chat Moss near Warrington. The water company have called this the Kew Outflow and huge muscular pipes carry water from one deep ditch to another, metal grills allowing water through but collecting litter, bags, branches. The hum of machinery, the rush of brown foamy water full of grass and leaves: not for the first time on the old mosses I felt that the water was being monitored and kept in check but that it could rise and drown this land again, as it has done before.

The railway line is long dismantled but the land retains its footprint. The line ran along a drainage ditch towards the incline of the Kew Embankment and the grey gasometer in Meols Cop on the horizon, but nothing remains of the track bed here today; the eye makes leaps of faith and suggests links and junctions where none exist. Behind, the trackbed footprint is more visible and curves gently away towards Shirdley Hill. Down the artificial hill from the railway bridge, Heathey Lane makes an abrupt left turn to run across the fields of Jack's Mere and join the main road at the handsome St Mark's church. Across the T-junction the road is quieter as it runs through the dormitory village of Shirdley Hill and Renacres Moss, a stubble-brown land of fields and smoky trees. Shirdley Hill is marked on many old maps, and is possibly an ancient settlement, although nothing of any age seems to survive today. Until the 1930s it had a railway station on the Altcar Bob line and the site is marked by roads of bungalows commemorating Thomas Shaw, one of the stationmasters, but the station and the railway line are long gone. The village is quiet during the day, and walking through it I saw nobody but horses and watchful cats. Beyond the village the fields opened up again and the view was greater, the land beginning to curve softly; presumably this gentle swell is Shirdley Hill itself. The road was lined with hedges of beech, the copper leaves rattling in the cold wind, and led me past the mission church of St Aidan, a simple church hall of a building, the roof mossy and stained with lichen, a foundation stone marking a ceremony of dedication in 1925. The farms here are arable, and the cold air carried the winter-vegetable smells of leeks and Brussels sprouts. The church spire at Halsall was rising clear of its trees across the muddy fields, the ruts of water reflecting a silver-grey sky. The land was becoming gently rolling, with low hills, and at the private hospital of Renacres Hall the fields looked less industrial, more broken by spinneys and hedges. Across the fields the redundant Altcar Bob railway bridge at New Cut Lane appeared as a grey arch on the much larger Halsall Moss.

The land dropped gently through woods and past farm buildings, Brook House Farm and (on the map at least) the strangely Germanic Wolden Haus, near a small brook and a thin stand of beech trees. Across the main Halsall road was Morris Lane, with more farms and the small cottages of Victorian farm workers, and here the road rose over the canal on a narrow stone bridge. This was the Leeds–Liverpool Canal, and many of the small whitewashed cottages between here and Pinfold/Scarisbrick date from the very early years of the 19th century – 1806, 1807 – perhaps indicating an increase in building that coincided with the canal delivering visitors to Southport. Softened by time and nature, the canal seems a part of the landscape, the stonework attractively weathered, the water home to reeds and fish; but I wonder how this industrial intrusion was seen in the mid-18th century. On the sharp bend where Morris Lane becomes Pinfold Lane, the stubble was golden and was being picked over by a small flock of partridges. All the buildings in the pretty village of Pinfold in Scarisbrick date from the time that the Southport tourist trade was starting to become important to the canal: 1792, 1796, 1807, 1809, 1821. The houses are solid and made of grey-yellow sandstone, and perhaps some were built as shops, or small guest houses, accommodation for canal workers or carters. The old road from Southport to Ormskirk was roaring with traffic after the quiet of the fields, but it runs under an avenue of chestnuts. The red-golden leaves had all fallen but the pavement and hard-muddied verges were lined with dusty, faded conkers. A cock pheasant and a harem of hens were feeding in the fields, almost invisible against the stubble on this misty afternoon.

I had come to see the Red Lion bridge at Pinfold/Scarisbrick, as it was here that the slow boats from Manchester unloaded their tourists for the horse carriages that would take them across the Moss to Southport. The old Red Lion pub on the canal was closed and being transformed into an Indian restaurant. From the towpath on other side of the bridge I could see a large 'lay-by' on the canal, a pregnant bulge in the canal wall for turning boats, perhaps the very spot where the Georgian visitors disembarked to be met by William Sutton's carts.

The road to Ormskirk and the motorway is noisy and always busy, but the canal was full of narrowboats and pleasure craft and a faded poster beneath Red Lion Bridge mapped out local sites of interest. This landscape has had the pull of tourism *versus* industry since Southport's earliest days, when local fishermen carried giggling society girls to the sea for bathing, and farm workers were hired to transport visitors to and from the canal in smartened farm wagons. I found earlier layers of history in the suggestion on the poster of the drained mediaeval landscape; it pointed me to a wayside cross on Black Moss Lane, which I couldn't find. I had more luck with the large Scarisbrick Wayside Cross in the wall of Scarisbrick Hall, a survivor of two lines of pre-Reformation land marking. From Scarisbrick, tracks marked by stone crosses lead to Burscough Priory and Ormskirk church, allowing safe travel across what was then a dark, boggy wilderness and a meditative landscape; the crosses were used for prayer on the long journey of a funeral procession. Burscough's great priory has disappeared, leaving only an 'abbey lane' and two huge crumbling pillars of stone in a field near a caravan site, and Scarisbrick Cross has lost its Christ-figure and one of its arms. It is hidden from the road and drifted with leaves, but the road it marked still carries modern traffic to Ormskirk.

Burscough Priory.

Scarisbrick Hall is now a private school, but the thin mock-mediaeval tower is a local landmark and visible for miles around. The park has a thick belt of woodland around it, full of golden beech leaves on this smoky, cold afternoon. The landscape along Black Moss Lane, by contrast, is agricultural on an industrial scale, with large farm-factory buildings seeming to swallow an old farmhouse in the trees like a snake swallowing a frog; the road verges are churned and rutted by lorries. Beyond, the land rises past Ellen's Home Farm and Black Moss Farm, a small plaque commemorating 'Marquis and Marquesa de Casteja 1878', the second farmhouse in half a mile to bear a dedication to these Spanish aristocrats, who were once the inheritors of Scarisbrick Hall. The public footpath runs alongside the fields, but in contrast to the heavily worked fields the path is neglected and badly signposted, and the grass is long and wet. Again, the land has memories of water; on the map at least, Black Moss gives way to Jack's Mere and the footpath turns across the fields towards Renacres Moss and the road back towards Southport. Turfland is a company growing turf for golf courses and hotel lawns on the old lake beds; the public footpath runs across this lawn of clipped grass, but it seemed too neat for footsore travellers and an unsuitable place for my wet, muddy boots. With the light fading, I followed the path back towards Shirdley Hill to rejoin Heathey Lane and the road into Southport.

Before I began to explore the old mosses I had very much taken them for granted. The farms seemed industrial, the land flat and uninteresting. But I grew very fond of this old landscape with its lost trails, dusty roads, stories of giant elk and mediaeval pilgrim routes. I found it a very beautiful place, full of birds and wild flowers as well as industrial farm machinery. And quite apart from the language of modern land drainage, with its canals and ditches and cuts, I found it beautiful and poetic that the lost watery landscape is still there in the place names. There are many Brook Houses, Mere Farms and Moss Farms. Martin Mere's dimensions are suggested by Mere Brow and Mere Side. Above all, the old mosses and meres – White Moss, Black Moss, Jack's Mere – are marked on modern Ordnance Survey maps, and so may still be used as reference points nearly 400 years after they were first drained.

CHAPTER TWO

VICTORIAN SUBURBIA

When Queen Victoria came to the throne in 1837 Southport was in its infancy, but by the time she died in 1901 the layout and street pattern was more or less established as the town we know today. This is true of many British towns and cities, and I have thought for a long time that modern Britain is essentially a country built by the Victorians. Many of us live in Victorian houses, and in any town the railway stations, schools, churches, town halls and even hospitals are often 19th-century buildings. They are so commonplace, so familiar, as to be almost invisible, and are therefore still easily lost to redevelopment. For this reason I have long had a fascination with Victorian landscapes, a love of Victorian churches, school buildings and cemeteries, and I am especially attracted to the forgotten places, the overlooked back streets, the crumbling churches, the derelict houses. I am fascinated by streetscapes, how the streets are made, the cobblestones and manhole covers, and I love the way the Victorians handled landscape; in Southport they built long straight roads, but they dealt with urban necessities very well.

This chapter grew from notes made on long walks across one of my favourite parts of Southport, the miles of Victorian suburbia running east from Chapel Street. This is the town that the visitors never see. I wanted to acquaint myself with it, to see familiar buildings from new angles, to discover where streets went and how they connected to places I knew. I found a wholly different town by quiet afternoons of suburban exploration, sometimes with other walkers, photographers, writers or artists, but usually alone, following my nose down quiet sunny streets from Churchtown to Birkdale. Southport is largely a flat town, and makes for easy walking. The walks usually lasted four or five hours and were followed by an hour writing up my notes in an empty pub never visited before or since, the sunlight streaming through onto a threadbare carpet, looking back over the photographs in the digital camera, a record of the journey in street names, manhole covers and unusual buildings. I could happily spend the rest of my life on such journeys.

It is strange to think that most houses in Southport were built before World War One. All the rigidity of Victorian and Edwardian social life can be seen in them, from the grand detached houses built around Hesketh Park to the small working-class homes built in Kew. The larger villa properties in Birkdale Park, Scarisbrick New Road or around Hesketh Park have often survived in reasonably good condition, even though they were built for the comfort of one family and made to be run by servants and for decades have been too big to be inhabited in this way. Many were broken up into flats, and with the new demand for sleek city-centre living, many now are being renovated again, transformed into modern urban flats in a Victorian shell. Some were also big enough to be converted into retirement homes or prestigious offices, their grounds big enough to park cars and yet retain lawns, borders and fine trees. A century or more after planting, these trees are in their maturity, and they both screen the houses from the road and provide a frame for the houses as they were intended to do. These large houses intrigue and delight me, but they are not to everybody's taste. Birkdale Park and

Abandoned gates in Birkdale – modern victoriana.

Hesketh Park are reasonably conservative in their architecture, but Scarisbrick New Road in particular has many examples of the experimentation of the Victorians, what many people regard as the crass and ugly side of Victorian taste – a steep roof with the Southport trademark crown of filigree ironwork, half-timbered gables echoing Tudor manor houses, a sturdy pair of classical Birkdale houses, with arched windows and heavy stone window frames.

Smaller detached villas have fared very badly over the last 30 years or so, as these buildings no longer have any purpose. The largest of these houses, on roads like Portland Street or Hawkshead Street, have been turned into retirement homes, but generally they are too big to be modern houses and too small to be adapted to other uses. The lucky ones have been divided into flats and maintained, their plasterwork and floorboards kept well-painted and polished, but most have been divided cheaply and without love. Most in fact now seem to be divided into bedsits and flats, or are serving as offices. Their front gardens, which once would have had clipped hedges, mown grass and beds of small colourful flowers, have often been paved over for cars, or just driven over so that the garden is lost and the ground is muddied. Thirty years after they were paved the concrete is crumbling and the weeds come through, the paving tilts, the weeds flower and set seed, the paving suffers still further. Some smaller villas were clad in fake Lakeland stone in the 1970s, when carriage-lamps appeared and ageing brick walls were rebuilt with breeze blocks. As their owners took no interest in the history or appearance of the houses, Victorian sash windows were replaced with modern neo-Georgian bull's eyes, walls were demolished, and the gardens used for storing rusty vans and lengths of pipe. These houses are still imposing but neglected and distressed, yet on once-grand roads such as Portland Street the names of some survive; Springfield carved into the sandstone wall, so deeply that years of paint cannot obliterate it, Stoneleigh found carved into a gatepost in a wall with no gate, Belvedere, still over the front door. Even the smaller houses had names, and on Cemetery Road there are Victoria Villas, built in 1897, the year of Victoria's Diamond Jubilee, Rose Villas, Primrose Bank, and Daisy Bank, assertions of rural individuality as the town roads spread across the fields and sand dunes. Ash Street has another Belvedere and Desney House, and a fine collection of Victorian gateposts – knocked, moved but still a solid presence, the deep fine carving overpainted with numbers and directions. Springfield, Belvedere, Primrose Bank: empty Victorian names long out of use for these buildings.

In 1865 Southport laid out a city for the dead. Duke Street Cemetery was laid out along Snuttering Lane, ancient Churchgate, which became Cemetery Road, and was connected to the town centre by the long straight run of Duke Street itself. It is still a very beautiful graveyard, laid out on a series of avenues and half-moon junctions, the older part attractively landscaped with mature trees. The oldest avenues are not grand

Above, below and facing page: Stonework and silhouettes in Duke Street Cemetery.

Ornate and highly attractive ironwork; Cemetery Road gateway.

Above and below: The monument to the crew of the Eliza Fernley, *Duke Street Cemetery.*

and are a little unkempt, allowing flowers and ivy to grow across the tombs. I do not believe that cemeteries should be too neat, and the grounds are obviously well-maintained; a little greenery softens the grief, adds dignity to old stone, perhaps reassures us. I have an affinity with Victorian cemeteries, perhaps because their world seems so different from ours, their beliefs so different. I love the formality of the lodge houses, the mortuary chapels, the clock tower. Family graves remembering a soldier from World War One I find especially poignant, but to my mind the most interesting monuments are the older ones, the ones erected by mourning widowers and sorrowful widows at the end of the 19th century. Many of the stones record the towns that people left to live in Southport, such as Reigate, Waterford, Scarborough and Wigan; or perhaps they had holiday homes here. Many of the grander tombs record the names of houses – Elsinore, Beechwood, Larkfield – which is interesting to my eyes as many of these house-names have been superseded by simple numbers; but there is also the uneasy suggestion that even now these dead Victorians are seeking to impress us. These overblown Gothic memorials, sheered columns, draped urns and above all angels seem to have a drama lacking in the modern gravestones in the bare field beyond, with their simple black marble stones and gold lettering; or perhaps I don't feel as comfortable examining modern graves with such enthusiasm. Possibly the most tragic memorials in

a seaside town are those to the seamen and master mariners lost at sea, but most moving of all is the memorial to the life-boatmen who died in the *Mexico* disaster in 1886. On a grassy island of its own the monument is surrounded by greenery and birdsong, and the council has provided a bench; it is a quiet place, a thoughtful Southport place. This solid granite monument on its sandstone base is more like a public monument than a tomb, more proud and commemorative now than grieving. The stone waves on top have drowned the broken mast and seem to threaten to overspill the monument itself. The heavy granite sides are decorated with plaques which record the tragedy, and the panel showing the *Eliza Fernley* finally overcome by the waves has become softened by time, giving the monument the look of an ivory casket.

The cemetery stops short of the fields with a six-foot-high drop, a town wall for Southport. This is

Art Nouveau Gothic window, Portland Street.

the very edge of the town, with only fields beyond, although in the last 20 years or so more houses and roads have been built at Kew. Furthest away from Cemetery Road there is a large Jewish section, separated from the Christian graves by an odd wall of crumbling 1950s concrete posts. Many of the Jewish graves seem cut from white marble, sooted slightly after 30 years or so. The names of the dead are carved with both English words and Hebrew script, common-era dates and Jewish dates, many of which tally with the 1930s and 1940s, a sharp reminder of the different lives of European Jews at that time. The Jewish cemetery is a quiet place, full of birdsong, and recent visitors have placed pebbles on the graves of loved ones, a beautiful and gently poignant Jewish tradition. I was reminded of other Jewish cemeteries I have seen, in Nice and Prague, which gave this little corner of Southport a cosmopolitan air. The only flowers are in the marshy ground below the wall or on the large unused cemetery field next door, which is dotted with daisies, buttercups and dandelions and, as there is nothing between here and the open spaces of Town Lane, there are many birds. At this far end of Duke Street there is another of Mr Webb's Patent Sewer Gas Destructors, the second or third I found on my walks across the town, standing like a derelict lamp-post, overpainted and rusting.

Duke Street Cemetery is surrounded by the smaller semi-detached houses built for the middle and working classes, which are the most visible Victorian houses in Southport. There is a huge crescent of them sweeping through the town from Tithebarn Road and Hart Street to Kew Road and Bedford Park.

Rust and peeling paint, Cemetery Road.

36

Many of these houses were built in lots by speculative builders, who would often live in the first house they built while the others were being erected. Some were rented for considerable periods of time; sometimes a single family would stay in a house for decades, paying rent to a succession of new owners. We bought our Southport house from a family in Gloucestershire, and I think that decorating and gently renovating this Victorian house gave me a new appreciation of the layers of history in these old houses, peeling back 1950s wallpaper and carpets to discover old floorboards, Victorian pennies under skirting boards, the ghost lines of long-gone dado rails.

What must the town have been like when these streets were being built? Great numbers of houses in Southport and Birkdale seem to have been built from the 1870s to the late 1890s, and large areas of the town must have felt like one big building site. A century has softened these roads, but back then everything was being built at the same time, the roads and drains laid out, the plots being developed. The houses were built of brick, sometimes with a crisp engineering brick being used for the façades of the houses and more ordinary common brick for the backs and side walls. The roofs were of Welsh slate, and I think the miles of slate roofs are one of the most attractive aspects of the Southport skyline. Many of these houses still have simple terracotta baskets of fruit or abstract designs over the front doors, and sometimes an elaborate pattern of terracotta brick beneath the eaves, suggestive of Indian designs. Blue engineering brick and strings of yellow terracotta tiles were used to break the red-brick façade, and painted sandstone was used for windowsills and door frames. The porches were small but had a welcoming floor of tiles suggesting a carpet, and sometimes a wall dado of tiles as well, perhaps echoing the tiled 'cheeks' of Victorian fireplaces. The front door often had a large central stained-glass window and perhaps two smaller lights above, and many of these smaller front-door windows survive across the town. Perhaps because of my interest in Victorian churches, I love stained glass; it throws a warm light into the hallway during the day and shines out into the road at night, and I was pleased to discover that there are still companies in Southport specialising in domestic stained glass. The rest of the windows were in wooden sash frames which lifted vertically, helped by weights on ropes hidden in the heavy framework. The surviving Victorian glass is not as uniform as modern glass, and gives a delicately imperfect view of the world outside; the ripples repeat in the sunshine, and in many cases have thrown a watery square of light onto the walls for a hundred years.

The hallway often had a 'lincrusta' dado of thick paper with low-relief decoration, apparently manufactured by just one company, a firm called Lincrusta-Walton on Tyneside. In cheaper houses the front door led straight into the parlour, but in more expensive homes the hall led to the staircase and had simple plasterwork decoration, perhaps wall coving and a ceiling rose around the central light fitting. Many of these

Redundant house names in Southport.

houses would be lit by gas but towards the end of the century they were being fitted with electric light. Downstairs, the front room or parlour was often kept for best, with perhaps a piano and family portraits or photographs, aspidistras and antimacassars, little lacy confections to keep the hair-oil off the furniture. This public room sometimes had a bay window, especially in later or more expensive houses. Every room except the pantries and sculleries would have had a cast-iron fireplace, although the ones in the bedrooms upstairs were often unlit; some of these bedrooms had never been heated before central heating was installed in the 1960s or 1970s. The second room downstairs was a dining room or more commonly a kitchen, with a large cast-iron range used for cooking, baking and boiling water. This was the heart of the house, with a large kitchen table for meals and family activities. There might be a small scullery with a large sink and the water supply, used for washing dishes and pots and pans. The larger semi-detached houses often had a smaller pantry leading off this 'back kitchen', and a separate wash house outside was reached from the back yard, which might have its own fireplace and a large 'copper' for boiling clothes. There was no indoor toilet and the WC was a small separate building in the yard. All houses in Southport were originally built with a garden, or at least some outside space to grow a few flowers or vegetables. The front gardens in the late 19th century were not radically different from some modern gardens, with a small lawn and borders full of bedding plants, and perhaps a privet hedge planted by the builder.

The streets were cobbled with hard stone cobbles or setts, and had kerbstones of granite or sandstone. Many had pavements of square blue tiles, a flooring material not used in southern Lancashire but common up the Fylde coast. Some can still be seen in Birkdale or on Lord Street. The streets would have been lit by cast-iron lamp-posts, and all the street furniture and ornament, from manhole covers to bollards, would have been made of cast-iron. Perhaps these streets of semi-detached houses looked their best 30 or 40 years after they were built, when they would have been fully occupied and personalised by individual taste, and the trees on the wealthier streets would have been mature. Left alone and well maintained, these houses age well; their red-brick walls age to a softer colour and the hard shine is worn off the blue/red floor tiles by a century of pedestrians, although the paintwork needs painting more often than on inland buildings as it fades quickly in the salt air.

These Victorian and Edwardian houses started to fall out of fashion after World War Two. With increased prosperity and more consumer goods, they began to be too small for modern needs and they suffered much the same fate as the larger houses on Ash Road or Portland Street. The houses between Portland Street and Southbank Road are small and tatty, cottagey but overgrown and crammed full of junk; many of the smaller houses in Southport seem to be overflowing with possessions, almost too small for human habitation. Ordinary people began to be able to afford cars, and many of the front gardens in streets like Kew Road began to be sacrificed to park them off the road. Kitchen equipment changed and people cooked on smaller, more efficient cookers; the old kitchen became a dining room, or had the wall between it and the parlour demolished to make one big room downstairs. More kitchen space was needed for refrigerators, washing machines, freezers; the solution was to enlarge the kitchen by demolishing the pantry wall, or perhaps to extend under the stairs.

The housing ideal became a home on a new estate with a garden for the children, and a driveway and garage for the car. As attitudes to housing changed, the old houses began to be seen as 'starter homes', fit only for young people starting married life together. The new owners' grandparents would have raised four or five children in one of these houses, but increasingly they were seen as too small for more than one child, and merely a step on the ladder to the suburbs proper and a modern house. With the new 1970s home style of sleek lines and bright colours, everything possible was done to deny that these houses were nearly a century old, and many of them were radically transformed. Their subtle brick and terracotta decoration was plastered over and then pebble-dashed, their sash windows were torn out and cheap wooden or plastic doors and windows installed. Even the town authorities joined in; both street and pavement

These Victorian houses look their best when maintained rather than given new windows and doors.

Above and below: modern Victorian streets in Southport.

were often simply covered with tarmac in the 1960s, but the old stone cobbles or blue tiles occasionally resurface during repair work. Walking past during such work in 2004 I saw the old cobbles on Vaughan Road, off Eastbourne Road, but after the repairs the old surface was quickly covered with a thick layer of tar again. On many of these streets only the chimneys survived; too high to reach easily and in any case made unnecessary by central heating, they were simply left where they were. Across its Victorian and Edwardian suburbs Southport has a silent tilting forest of redundant chimney pots.

But tastes change, and attitudes to these old houses shifted from the 1980s, when people came to a new appreciation of Victorian domestic taste. Estate agents began to talk of 'original features' and older aspects of the houses were sometimes restored; they were then perhaps a century and a half old and had as much history as any castle. To the bemusement of their parents, who remembered these houses as damp and cold, the new owners threw out the carpets and had the old floorboards stripped and varnished, replaced fireplaces, restored plasterwork. Chimneys were swept and fires relit, for the first time in 40 or 50 years. The ugly 1970s flagstones were torn up, the brickwork was cleaned and repointed, and more sensitive materials such as stone and cobbles were used to provide a parking space. The small gardens given to each house by law in the 1880s were seen as ideal for 'low maintenance' town gardening – perhaps a terrace and a few pots of plants, room for a table and chairs, ideal for a barbecue and a glass of wine. But it is true that these small Southport houses have suffered the most of all the town's Victorian housing stock. Far too many of Southport's old houses have been badly treated over the years, and sadly it seems to me to be a question of money. The larger houses have survived with dignity, but the smaller the house, the more likely it is to have been gutted and remodelled with the modern horrors of pebble-dashing, swirly plaster on internal walls and ceilings, plastic windows and doors, ugly concrete paving and breeze-block walls.

What does the future hold for Southport's Victorian suburbs? Without doubt the biggest change since they were laid out is car ownership; families are generally smaller but more people own cars than ever before. On old photographs even small streets look wide and empty, but today they are lined with motor cars. This is not just Southport's problem, of course. The larger semi-detached properties and villas can absorb paved space for car parking in the grounds, but the smaller houses in many cases have lost front gardens and look intimidated by large modern vehicles. But if these car parking problems could be solved and the houses treated with a little more respect, then these long streets could take their rightful place as a part of Southport's Victorian heritage, and perhaps one day visitors will regard the residential districts as worth exploring in their own right.

CHAPTER 3

BESIDE THE SEASIDE

I used to think that Southport was torn between the sophistication of Lord Street and the more low-brow attractions of the seafront, but they now seem like two sides of the same coin. The town was built for pleasure, and the fantasy architecture of the town centre is just a different expression of this. I like to think of tired Edwardian visitors walking home to one of the hotels on Lord Street after a hard day's racing up and down the sands or shrieking on a fairground ride, the feet of sleepy children leaving sandy trails in the deep carpet. The town offered holidaymakers many types of holiday experience, from shopping and donkey rides to sleeping in a Gothic tower in the Prince of Wales Hotel.

'Crop circle' tyre tracks made by Land Rovers at Southport Pier.

And there is a long tradition of seaside fun at Southport. Long before the establishment of the town, the parishioners of North Meols celebrated Big and Little Bathing Sundays, when the wide sands would be filled with people willingly entering the sea for pleasure or at least custom. 'The shore is thronged with several hundred extra visitors,' wrote F.W. Robinson in 1848, 'there are bathing machines at a premium, donkeys brisk, and boats inclined for sail.' He describes these extra visitors as 'rustics', as they were largely country people following a pleasurable tradition older than the town itself. But they would not have regarded the sea as a playground. It provided food and income, but it was a dangerous place and there are many memorials to drowned fishermen along this coast. It became fashionable for the middle classes to bathe in the sea at the end of the 18th century, and Southport's founding legend has it that the innkeeper William Sutton took advantage of this trend. People were increasingly visiting the area in order to bathe in the sea, and Sutton arranged donkey carts to carry them from the inn at Churchtown to the good sands at South Hawes. In 1792 he opened a rough-and-ready shelter to allow the bathers to change into and out of bathing clothes. This was in a sheltered spot near a stream in the sandhills, at the southern end of the long shallow valley that would become Lord Street. But it is probable that Sutton was not the first to take advantage of this trade; local cottagers and fishermen were also taking in visitors, and Belle Vue Cottage was built in 1797, which took in paying guests. Sutton was spurred on to build the Original Hotel near to his bathing shelter, on the banks of the small river later known as the Nile, which he perhaps used as a supply of fresh water. The Original Hotel and Belle Vue Cottage were followed by a number of other grand cottages and places to stay which were built along the shallow valley. It is from these beginnings that Southport is said to have grown. The town was popular for residents and visitors almost immediately, and buildings began to spread over the remote landscape of sand dunes and valleys. Southport was well established as a seaside holiday town by the time the railways arrived in 1848.

What must it have been like, to have stayed in Sutton's hotel and bathed in the sea in the late 1790s? The Original Hotel was in an isolated place in the sandhills, with Churchtown the nearest settlement apart from the scattered cottages of Birkdale. Guests would have arrived in the town on horseback or carriage from the canal at Scarisbrick, to Roe Lane and the long valley of 'Lord Street'. The Botanic Gardens Museum has an amazing recreation of a room in Sutton's Original Hotel; it seems to have been a dark place, lit by candles or oil lamps, the walls made of wood, the floorboards creaking, like an 18th-century sailing ship. Several of Sutton's possessions have survived and are on display. It is possible to touch one of the large chests of drawers from the Hotel, a link with the holiday visitors of two centuries ago. The Hotel's large earthenware beer jugs are on show alongside Sutton's violin and his pipe.

The earliest seaside pleasures – bathing machines and fishing boats in the 1860s.

The giant sand yachts, once a common sight on the sands at Southport.

More sedate yachting in the 1950s.

A Victorian fisherman 'putting' for shrimps with a wide net.

Shrimps were also caught by 'cart shanking' from a small cart. In the background of both pictures are the fishing boats working in deeper water.

Even one of the Hotel ledgers has survived, with accounts for 1802 in William Sutton's handwriting. The earlier changing shelter was assembled from driftwood and the planks from wrecked ships, but drawings show the Original Hotel as a more sophisticated and conventional building, which seems to have been renovated and extended over the course of its 60-year history. The bathing shelter and Sarah Walmesley's Belle Vue Cottage could have been seen from the hotel, in a landscape not

so different from the sand dunes and valleys at Ainsdale and Birkdale today, with paths through the sand hills to the beach and the sea. The coastline was suitable for bathing because of the wide flat sands, and bathing machines and huts for visitors to change their clothes would perhaps have sat at the high tide mark.

To walk from Lord Street out to the seafront and the pier is to walk backwards and forwards through time. For decades the sea has been retreating, and the town has built new seafront attractions to compensate; in the 1860s the waters lapped at the Promenade, where the flower beds of King's Gardens are today. Perhaps some of this is reversed as the cheaper seaside pleasures are now to be found a stone's throw from Lord Street, on the approach roads of Scarisbrick Avenue and Nevill Street. Scarisbrick Avenue sees itself as a commercial 'micro-village', with arches over the entrances to the avenue and a grand sign advertising its historical links and seaside attractions. It has plenty of bright, colourful shops selling seaside treats such as candy floss and sticks of rock, buckets and spades, windmills, and hopefully 'kiss me quick' hats and flags for sandcastles. There are traditional cafés and old-fashioned fish and chip restaurants, cheerful businesses which are a vital part of the English seaside tradition. But at the

William Sutton's Original Hotel in the dunes near the boundary with Birkdale.

Left: Traditional pleasures and modern security.

time of writing Scarisbrick Avenue is a dismal, scruffy place. Many of the buildings are run down and almost derelict, with empty shop fronts, broken windows, and filthy doorways smelling of urine. And ironically they were very attractive, unusual Victorian buildings with oriel windows and stained glass, and floors of apartments above. Light falls from broken leaded windows onto carved banisters and scuffed floorboards. The

The Victorian promenade on a quiet but sunny day in 1856. Note the bathing machines on the sands.

The end of the pier in 1860, showing the elegance that the Victorians brought to functional structures.

crossroads with West Street has smart terracotta façades, but here too the buildings are neglected and dirty. The best that can be said about Scarisbrick Avenue is that there are big plans to renovate it, and that it leads to the Promenade.

Here the landscape opens up after the narrowness of Scarisbrick Avenue. The white stucco hotels curve away along the road, and in front are the flower beds and hedges of King's Gardens. Nathaniel Hawthorne lived here for a time in the 1850s, and was visited by Herman Melville, arriving in Liverpool after a long sea voyage. Hawthorne was a passionate town explorer, and often went on long nocturnal walks across the towns he lived in. I like to imagine these giants of American literature exploring Southport together, walking and talking along the Promenade; I see Hawthorne as detached and calm, Melville as excited and passionate. When they walked here the sea reached the Promenade, and the sands would have stretched out in front of them; if buildings had memories then perhaps the old hotels would remember sand yachts, bathing machines and beach huts. A darker aspect of seaside life is recalled in the neat granite and bronze of the lifeboat memorial, with its plea to remember the lifeboatmen who have died over the years. There are always flowers on the monument whenever I walk past.

In the 1930s Fortunio Mantania painted a Venetian carnival on the Marine Lakes in King's Gardens, one of a series of works he painted to attract visitors to the resor'

Ironwork and stained glass on Scarisbrick Avenue.

Will some kind
hand please place
a flower on
this Obelisk
in honour of all
LIFEBOATMEN

The lifeboat memorial on the Promenade. The request is usually answered.

Elegant people dressed as pierrots talk and flirt in the gardens at night, illuminated by globe-lamps on columns rising from the balustrades and strings of lights reflected in the water. The picture suggests calm warm nights, sophistication, perhaps the possibility of romance. I like the idea of seeing a park as a place for illumination and night-time parties – a landscape, perhaps the whole town, created for glamour, rather as London sometimes seems a stage set for royal processions. Mantania would work hard to find any glamour in King's Gardens today. Much of the ironwork is rusty, the bushes are overgrown and unkempt, the paintwork all needs a fresh coat and at least one of the globe-lamps has been replaced with a black plastic bin bag, presumably to protect the electrics inside the column. This basic maintenance should be done every winter, especially if Southport wishes to remain a 'classic resort' and attract Britain in Bloom commendations for the quality of its public gardens. King's Gardens were a disappointment and I felt that the town lets itself down in not maintaining them to a higher standard.

King's Gardens are, however, in good condition compared to the neglected spaces behind them. At one time the globe-lamps illuminated a wide boardwalk through King's Gardens and over the Marine Lakes to Prince's Gardens, which were opened by the Prince of Wales in 1921. A sweeping classical colonnade led the eye through a small

Genteel net curtains, Sacrisbrick Avenue. Traditional seaside pleasures – but the café behind them has closed.

arched building, which carried visitors into the open space beyond and the sea-bathing lake which stood on the seaward side of the Gardens. All this has gone. The path now stumbles to a halt at a small modern café building which looks as though it has been recently attacked. Patches of concrete have been damaged, rubbish is stored alongside it and the ventilation grilles are blackened with smoke and grease. The park behind consists of nothing more than a large open field, which has been used by joy riders and is rutted and muddy. There is no attempt at landscaping or gardening. In place of the sea baths is Ocean Plaza, a modern shopping mall development of shops, cinema, restaurant and hotel. No care has been taken to align this development with the park landscape behind it, and the whole looks carelessly thrown onto the seafront. Would it have been more difficult or more expensive to site the new mall properly, to allow a long graceful pedestrian avenue from the old Promenade through the two parks and to the seafront? In 1995 Harry Foster wrote: 'The whole sea-front area was a harmonious tribute to municipal planning and development.' It was, but is no longer. This lack of urban grace could perhaps be forgiven if Ocean Plaza made an elegant contribution to the town's skyline, but it is a curiously sterile complex, low and unobtrusive compared to the previous century's collection of seafront hotels and towers.

The fairground rides of Southport were once erected on the beach in front of the Promenade, but are now confined to Pleasureland, next to Ocean Plaza on the seafront. This is the other side to the resort, a bright ghetto of tinsel glamour and romance far removed from the sophistication of Lord Street. I love this fairground element of the English seaside; snatching kisses from girls that taste of candy floss, the exhilarating

One of the smart modern entrances to the beach from the seafront. Muscular but as elegant as the Victorians' engineering.

nausea of the big dipper, the bone-shaking spins on the waltzers, the sense of freedom. Pleasureland is built in a strange pantomime Arabian Nights style, with 'Mustapha's Food Court', minarets and horseshoe arches around the doorways and a series of modern steel sculptures near the Lakeside Miniature Railway in King's Gardens. These are simple but surprisingly elegant, empty steel columns cut and opened like flowers, or like modern mosques. Pleasureland is a cocked snook to those who see Southport as a cut above, a place of only elegance, only cleanliness, but it has no mystery, nothing unexpected, and its seafront face is an unhappy mish-mash of peeling plaster walls, empty space and bad landscaping. And to my mind fairgrounds should be open fields for most of the year, apart from a fortnight of shrieking glamour, greasy food, thousands of light bulbs and non-stop rock 'n' roll. Perhaps even in a resort the fair should arrive in town like an invading army, huge gaudy trucks driven by surly, greasy teddy-boys, their sisters in bubble-gum pink and miles of petticoats. Pleasureland has none of this nostalgic glamour.

It is a sign of the times that the modern buildings of Pleasureland and Ocean Plaza face inland, and do not celebrate the glorious expanse of sand in front of them; we want you here, they seem to say, not sitting on the beach and saving your money. At least the council has recently renovated Marine Drive, and erected many handsome wind sculptures above the sweep of the sea wall. These creak and shift in the wind and seem to celebrate the natural cycle of the sea; stars, waves and shoals of fish. The beach at Southport is famous for its sheer size, with mile upon mile of hard, flat, dark-golden sand. The finest sand is next to the sea wall, presumably blown as far up the beach as possible by the breeze. The gold is mixed here with the bone white of shells, and the sand is soft underfoot. On the harder flat sand there are razor shells, winkles, and small crab shells, pieces of salt-polished wood, lumps of sea coal, perhaps washed up from the

The sculpture and carving on the waterfront celebrate the vast natural world of the seas – stars, fish, comets.

Wind sculptures on the seafront – they echo astrolabes and mechanical clocks, and move in the wind.

Strong modern sculpture on the Promenade commemorating the history of Southport's seafront. Once cyclists dived from the pier for the amusement of visitors.

The writhing coils of the modern rollercoaster, Pleasureland.

coal bins of a wreck. There is a piece of heavy ironwork standing proud of the sand about 300 yards off shore, which I had always wanted to see as I had assumed that it was the smokestack of a sunken ship. I was astonished to find that it was a tidal standard column, measuring the tides between Liverpool and Fleetwood in heavy Roman numerals – a beautiful object, rusted and smoothed by the sea and curious beachcombers.

Seaside trips should include a walk along the pier. The first pier at Southport opened in 1860, and was as long as the Promenade. It was a great success and was extended eight years later to a deeper channel 1,400 yards from the shore, which allowed pleasure steamers to link Southport with Anglesey and Barrow. The channels silted up over the years and the last steamer sailed in 1923, but Southport's pier has recently been overhauled and the views from the modern pier head are superb. Rivington Pike and Winter Hill can be seen inland, and on a bright January day snow can be seen on the Lake District fells. The smoky Welsh hills are visible far to the south, and occasionally on the horizon left of the Blackpool Tower the smudge of the Barrow fells appears, some 50 or 60 miles away. Southport itself is lost beneath the vast skies out here. A smudge of dune greenery, a slate roof, a handful of Victorian towers and 1960s flat roofs – from the end of the pier or from far out on the beach, this is all the town appears to be.

The modern pier pavilion is well designed and has the elegant clean lines of a terminal building for a small airport. There is a shop selling good-quality Southport souvenirs, and an exhibition of the town's history, wildlife and links with early aviation.

The dignified rusting ironwork of the tidal measuring device, Southport Sands. In the background is the sleek new pier pavilion.

On a sunny day it is a place of shimmering watery light, from the pools and wet sand flats below. I like spending a quiet hour here watching the birds feeding on the beach and lingering over a cup of tea; I am old enough now to be pleased that it comes in a proper ceramic mug and not a plastic cup. With the birds, the sand-pools, and the views towards Wales, I find the new pavilion a place for contemplation out of the cool breeze. But it is not a quiet place, as it also has many old penny-in-the-slot machines, which

The end of the pier – nothing between here and Ireland.

Traditional seaside treats after a day on the sands – candy floss and fudge, nougat and rock.

Older seaside pleasures photographed out of season.

fascinate modern children for their oddity. What the Butler Saw, Racing Trams, Slide-a-Penny – the pavilion is full of the clunks and clicks of mechanical toys in battered wooden and brass cases, the original lettering scraped and scuffed after a hundred years of end-of-the-pier amusement arcades and sticky fingers. I had thought that the machines would run on new money or metal discs the weight of old coins, but someone had the bright idea of installing change machines, new money for pre-decimal pennies. Every visit I sacrifice 10 new pence for the pleasure of buying an old penny, a permanent souvenir of half-an-hour spent drinking tea and watching shore birds feeding. How did it end up here, I wonder, this penny from 1962, this penny older than I am?

The walk back into town is dominated by the graceful triangle of the Marine Way Bridge, a splendid new crossing of the Marine Lakes, all concrete solidity and great tubular legs of steel, tethered with long steel ropes, an instant Southport landmark visible for miles. I like the new bridge and feels that it fits in with the mixture of old and new here. The white hotels on the distant promenade look out over the Marine Lakes, a place of low islands and rocky outcrops, winding pathways and shrubs. Unseen small birds whistle in the bushes and there are bigger birds out on the water: coots, swans, ducks and heavy geese. Yet this is also a modern, strangely American landscape, with Vue and Ocean Plaza to my right and the new shopping mall, hamburger restaurant and skateboard park on the left. There always seem to be old people here, perhaps merely curious or perhaps watching their grandchildren swirl and fly gracefully on their skates and boards up and over the ramps and inclines. This layering of the

Ideal holiday memories – Southport in the 1950s.

The Promenade and Old Pavilion, 1908.

Sunlight on the marine lakes and the whalebone arches of the restored pier.

generations is one of the pleasures of Southport, and no doubt the pensioners' grandparents looked upon their enthusiasms with similar loving bemusement. Many of Southport's older residents like the new pier, with its great views and smart shelters, and these are often full of well-dressed pensioners sharing a flask of tea, gossiping, reading or just gazing out to sea. New attractions like the skateboard park and the shopping mall have clearly outpaced the older seaside pleasures, and the Lakeside Miniature Railway below the pier is a shadow of its former self. The paint is peeling, the platforms are used for storing concrete slabs, the whole looks neglected and abandoned. In fact much of this newer, unfinished Southport around the pier is scruffy and unadopted, being gently colonised by salt-loving seashore plants, but there is a fascinating Victorian echo on this new land. The space beneath the pier, a place of struts and stones and black iron columns, has recently been coated with new topsoil, which seems to have come from a Victorian midden. The earth is full of large pieces of dinner plate, serving dishes and earthenware bottles, old bottles and medicine jars. The names of old potteries and the emblems of long-forgotten ceramics companies are still visible on broken plates and dishes. I recently spent an hour or so grubbing around here and came home with medicine phials, pieces of faded china, and green glass bottles emblazoned with the names of forgotten Southport companies.

A small train connects the pavilion with the Promenade and the new Silcock's Funland, a modern shed replacement for the old pier pavilion which stood here between 1902 and 1969, that dark year when Southport swept away much of the Victorian splendour of the town. Perhaps I am being hopeful and romantic in seeing the Moorish domes and secular minarets of the old building being reborn or surging

The old Pier Pavilion, demolished in 1969, photographed over a century ago.

The glorious whalebone arches of the pier. A new tram has since replaced the little train.

through in the new, in glossy plastic instead of iron and stained glass. There is another Victorian echo in front of the pavilion, the giant gallopers of the carousel, the painted horses silent, bright-eyed and watchful, safe under their permanent Big Top. It is a fitting terminal to the renovated Victorian pier. Older pier pleasures are also remembered in the sculptures along this stretch of the Promenade: the one-legged men and cyclists who used to dive off the pier into the sea, the shrimps for which Southport was famous. Made from coppery bronze and silver metals, these large and handsome sculptures improve the look of the street, like the wind sculptures on Marine Drive. Standing on the Promenade near the old white hotels, it is interesting to trace the journey the resort has made, from William Sutton's Original Hotel to the Victorian hotels, and through the amusement arcades of Nevill Street to the modern sculptures and Marine Way Bridge. It surprised me to realise that of course the older permanent attractions are still here, the simple pleasures that have brought visitors to this seaside resort for 200 years. Children still run on the beach, building sandcastles and finding driftwood. Families walk barefoot hunting for shells, talking and swinging their shoes. Old people sit on the pier and smile at sticky babies in pushchairs, youngsters sit on the sea wall flirting and laughing, and behind them the sea and the sky and the sand seem to roll on forever.

CHAPTER FOUR

LORD STREET

What would Southport be like without Lord Street? It is a startling and thought-provoking question, a 'what if?' question. What else could the town look like? How else could it be? Without Lord Street the town might have grown in a more haphazard fashion, the town centre roads would be more twisted, would turn more perhaps to go around the great sand dunes. The town might have evolved in a very different way, and instead of a grand boulevard, the heart of the town might be a maze of narrow streets connecting the shopping arcades with the Promenade and the seafront, a warren of alleys selling candy floss and cheap souvenirs. But perhaps without Lord Street there would be no shopping arcades, no long straight roads, no Promenade; perhaps the Victorians would have shown no interest in the town at all. Perhaps after a brief success as a Georgian seaside resort Southport would have shrivelled and died to become a Lancashire ghost town, with maybe a sad afterlife as the last station on the commuter trains from Liverpool if it survived that long. What is certain is that without Lord Street, Southport is almost inconceivable.

A Southport without this central avenue is unimaginable because this is where the town started, this is where it grew from; the geography of Lord Street defined early Southport, and some of the oldest buildings still survive here, built in the very earliest years of the 19th century when Lord Street was a valley in the sand dunes. Two hundred years later it still forms the spine and heart of the town; the major civic buildings of the town are on Lord Street – the town hall, the central library, the art gallery, as well as the department stores and the big hotels. There is so much here, so much of Southport on this one road, that I am sure that there are people who visit the town and never leave Lord Street. The towers and spires of Lord Street form much of Southport's horizon

The railway station, opera house and entrance to the Winter Gardens over a century ago.

when seen from Marshside or Crossens, as from one end to the other it is defined by landmark buildings. It is so grand that to call it a street seems inappropriate; if this one street is grand enough to make an impact on Southport's skyline, it should be at least an avenue, if not a boulevard.

The history of Southport can be read in the stones and bricks of Lord Street. It begins at the boundary with Birkdale, on the noisy roundabout that was once Nile Square. This is the heart of the earliest Southport stories, the oldest part of town. Sarah Walmesley's Belle Vue Cottage stood here, as did William Sutton's South Port Hotel. From these earliest stories Lord Street runs dead straight through all aspects of the town's history, past a Georgian terrace, the oldest hotels, the Victorian civic buildings, the grand banks, the ornate buildings serving as shops, the redundant but grand railway station, the lost footprint of the Winter Gardens and the sombre Monument to the town's military dead. It ends at a quiet roundabout where it meets the old road from Churchtown, but the line of the road runs on for another three-quarters of a mile or so into the suburbs around Hesketh Park.

Decaying ironwork on Cambridge Hall.

Part of Southport's charm is that relatively little is made of this grand road; there is no immediate sense that, as Peter Fleetwood-Hesketh says, this is one of the finest thoroughfares in the world. Lord Street is broad and well-proportioned and was designed well for both vehicles and pedestrians. The buildings are set far back from the roads, so that even with today's heavy traffic there is still a feeling of space, of openness. But because of this the charm of the street reveals itself slowly. Seeing it for the first time, it is the traffic that dominates, and the interesting architecture is not immediately apparent. A tower may be noticed, the impressive doorway to a bank, the glass awnings

Cambridge Hall roofline, silhouetted against the dawn.

Lord Street was for shopping and promenading – a view from the early 20th century.

and the shopping arcades, but on first glance not much else. Fantastic and richly varied they may be, but the buildings on Lord Street are only three storeys high, the pavements are usually very busy with shoppers and holidaymakers, and the view across the road is obscured with trees and traffic.

I think that Lord Street is at its best very early on a summer's morning, when the street is quiet and largely deserted, and the dominant sound is not engines but birdsong. The traffic is very light, just buses, the odd car and council vans collecting rubbish. Beams of sunlight catch the trees, dappling the stonework on the Monument or the Town Gardens Café. The trees are alive with birds, and the lawns and flowerbeds are full of blackbirds grubbing for insects in the cool sunshine. The only people on the streets seem to be lugubrious road sweepers with weathered faces, and women hurrying nervously to work. Linen is being delivered and collected from the great hotels, taxi drivers sit in their cars reading the papers and waiting for customers. There is a clatter as shutters are rolled up for the day and shop workers open up; wafts of a fresh warm bread smell drift across the street. I imagine the pots of coffee bubbling in the back rooms, the early staff gossiping and chatting about last night's television. As we stand on the Birkdale roundabout, the road stretches ahead of us, lined with trees, one side gently dominated by a great stone and brick tower. This is all that remains of Lord

Above and below: A Lord Street without people at 7am on a summer's morning.

Street Station, built in 1884 by the Southport & Cheshire Lines Extension Railway. This old gateway to the town is a Southport landmark, as are all the towers and spires of Lord Street, because of its height. It is an attractive building and I am glad that it has survived; station towers and church spires define a street and give perspective and distance to the urban landscape, and too many are lost once the building closes. The path through the clock tower leads to a car park and a supermarket, but the tower itself and the surviving station buildings are redundant and no use is made of the shops and offices.

Not all the landmark buildings of Lord Street are towers. Next to the old station is a very attractive 1920s building of warm brick with striking blue and white ornament on the windows, best appreciated from the other side of the road as the new activities on the ground floor ruin the symmetry of the building. This used to be the Garrick Theatre, and a small bronze plaque on the low pavement wall has David Garrick's face on it, smiling but slightly puzzled. The site was once occupied by Southport's Opera House and the Winter Gardens, so this small town block has seen great buildings come and go. The theatre was painted by Fortunio Mantania in 1935 as part of his series of works commissioned to advertise the town, and he saw the theatre in its prime. He painted the rich and famous emerging from an evening performance, the men in heavy overcoats, their wives in clinging silk dresses and fur stoles. Outside their chauffeurs wait patiently, and the lamps and tree-lights glimmer in the dark. The extreme ends of

The famous 'spire' of Cambridge Hall, surrounded by modern lighting and the attractive 'Coronation' light of 1953.

Lord Street are scruffier than the centre and today the Garrick is a bingo hall; the ground floor shops sell motorised bath chairs for old people, and discounted gifts and floor tiles. But the building has been well maintained and is still a landmark for Southport, where good buildings from this time stand out because of their rarity.

Lord Street still has elegant street lamps and tree-lights similar to those that Mantania painted, but only without the traffic it is really possible to appreciate how much greenery the street has. Southport is fortunate to have a busy shopping street of lawns, borders, flower beds and fountains; the inland side has the landmark towers and spires of the churches and civic buildings, as well as Wellington Terrace and the grandeur of the Prince of Wales Hotel, but it also has large gardens, bushes and shrubberies, and mature trees. Summer or autumn visitors take away an abiding memory of these trees, huge planes and chestnuts that spread over the pavement, and this great amount of greenery, stretching all the way along Lord Street, has kept the boulevard on a domestic scale; the street does not feel imposing or overpowering because one side of the road is almost invisible behind heavy trees and municipal gardens, and the great width of the road is not immediately apparent. The distance from building to building across Lord Street is nearly 90 yards, which would feel overpowering and authoritarian without the softening effect of the trees and gardens.

Lord Street is a very green boulevard, but it is renowned for its buildings. Southport is a town built for pleasure, and her buildings are attractive because of the element of fantasy. The buildings enhance the holiday mood, from the white Italianate hotels on the Promenade to the grandeur of Lord Street, where even banks and office buildings

Fortunio Mantania's painting of the Garrick Theatre, now in the Atkinson Art Gallery.

The spiky roofs of the Opera House, designed by Frank Matcham and lost in a fire in 1929.

The Garrick Theatre, an elegant replacement for the Opera House.

Columns, ironwork and quiet corners and Lord Street.

were built in an ornate fashion. The buildings on Lord Street are large and confident, perhaps florid to modern tastes but visually impressive; there seems a heavy frivolity about them. Nikolaus Pevsner described Lord Street as having a 'rewarding variety', a gentle way of saying, perhaps, that not all the buildings there are architectural gems. Some to me are ugly, but what astonishes is the simple fact that they have survived at

A faceless angel, Christ Church.

Ironwork on the bandstand, Lord Street.

all. Individually they would not stand out in any town centre; most British towns still have ornate Victorian banks or shops. But here they run for a mile or so in an almost continuous straight line, a dazzle of different architectural styles, different techniques, linked by the famous glass awnings with their ornate supporting columns. Fascinated by ornament and design, the Victorians borrowed ideas from all over the world and all periods of history, from ancient Rome to Gothic Europe, and the shops of Lord Street are a picture book of their enthusiasms. Some have no ancestors at all and are a product of the architect's vivid imagination, and the best have a host of fairy-tale elements stolen from nursery rhymes and legends; fantasy-Moorish windows from the Arabian Nights, classical temples, blue-tiled façades, heraldic beasts from an Arthurian castle. Opposite the real gardens there are gardens

An illuminated urn and fountains in the old Municipal Gardens, Lord Street.

of stone carved onto the façades; abstract swirls of foliage, heavy bunches of grapes or flowers. The shop buildings of Lord Street are a jumble of balconies and windows, and have a steep jagged roofline of balustrades, urns and imposing chimneys, dizzyingly steep roofs and crowns of filigree ironwork.

When the street was developed the stone animals and foliage would have been crisp and clean, the tiles and paintwork would have gleamed, the stained glass at night would have been magnificent. Perhaps we are too late to see them; they are weathered now, slightly mossy, neglected. The glass awnings are cracked or have been badly repaired and grass grows in the guttering, with dribbles of blood-red rust running down the thickly painted cast iron swirls. Banks have become wine bars. Stonework has become darkened by soot and neglect, the chimney pots are redundant, the stained-glass windows let light into dusty store rooms of boxes.

The reason for this is the changing commercial needs of the street. Lord Street is renowned for the quality and variety of its shops, and some have been in the town since the earliest days, but modern commercial premises change hands more quickly and have different security needs. Perhaps new tenants are only concerned with the shop front and the store rooms at the back. Certainly the rooms above, on two or three storeys, look neglected or even abandoned. But Lord Street is still the principal shopping district of Southport, and under the ageing glass awnings, protected from the rain and lit with a thin watery light on sunny days, are the best shops in town. The grand department stores are here, expensive clothes shops, places selling elegant shoes. The shops on Lord Street, like the buildings, are interesting for their variety, and next to the smart Italian shoes are bookshops selling publishers' clearance stock, and branches of national chains like Waterstone's, Next and Monsoon. But in Southport Waterstone's sells books in a beautiful and richly carved classical building of white stone, which I can rarely resist photographing on sunny days. Monsoon's clothing styles are displayed in a massive and dignified building of red polished granite, but not grand enough to stand out from the crowd on Lord Street.

There are charity shops raising money for incurable children, or adults with heart disease or cancer, and these bright, cheerful shops make a link with the older and more unusual places on the street. Elderly ladies who lunch can still be seen in jewellery shops and cafés that seem to have come straight from old Vienna; a world of fur coats, cream cakes and mahogany counters, the chandelier light glittering on gold necklaces and trays of rings and watches. Old signs indicate tobacco shops unchanged since the 1950s or advertise a history of commerce since 1848 or 1825 when Southport was only 30 years old.

The arcades of shops running from Lord Street are one of the glories of Southport. They gave shoppers even more protection from the weather than the glass awnings could provide, and also provided shortcuts across the town. The Royal Arcade is a warren of shops on two floors, the Cambridge Arcade has adapted to modern times and runs behind the library, but the greatest and most famous is the Wayfarer's Arcade. There are two storeys of shops, a great expanse of mosaic floor and huge lamps suspended from the great glasshouse roof. The shops sell fine furniture, shoes, clothes, elegant French goods and antiquarian books; it is certainly a splendid place to go shopping, yet for all its grandeur for some reason it has an air of melancholy.

To the walker rather than the shopper, Lord Street has more to offer than the endearing oddity of the buildings. Ignoring the disapproving glances of elderly women and uneasy shop assistants, I am drawn to the alleyways running between the blocks of shops. These are usually narrow, as if squeezed out by all the grandeur, and are perhaps the plain cousins of the grand arcades. Some are dull and utilitarian, yet they are often tiled with the attractive blue tiles that are found all over the town, and all lead to interesting places. Some connect with the small roads of warehouses and flats immediately behind the big roads, some run to tiny streets of three or four houses with overgrown gardens, silent and peaceful yet only two minutes from Lord Street. What must it be like to live on Lord Street yet see none of it? Some of these narrow paths lead to even narrower alleyways behind the shops, with brick walls that tower overhead, leaving only a strip of blue sky; greasy places for the shops' bins or the staff to have a smoke. Some of the alleyways have grand entrances, ornate tiled floors, yet are filthy and badly lit, and run through to a car park or another busy street. And there are invisible worlds here; some of these passageways run through to minute courtyards and

The famous glass awnings very early on a summer's morning.

The elegant street furniture and façades of Lord Street.

tiny restaurants almost invisible from Lord Street, but which have served Italian food or fish suppers for half a century.

Lord Street is lined with heavy wooden benches, and in all but the worst weather they are well used. Retired people sit here, eating sandwiches, waiting for a bus, reading newspapers or just resting, waiting for friends to walk past. Boys sit and jostle as they watch girls, and other young people on skateboards practise their moves and shuffles and wait to grow up. Perhaps this has always happened. This is the teenage Southport of street corners and school gangs, music shops and dreams of nightclubs with their unattainable sophistication, a strange place of graffiti, hamburgers, skateboard parks and perhaps the flashy, dark glamour of Pleasureland. Southport has excellent schools and leisure facilities, and an increasing number of fashionable bars and restaurants and smart clothes shops, but in general I think it has more to offer older people, and I would not like to grow up here. But the benches are a good place to watch the street, and the wide pavements are always crowded with shoppers, walkers, holidaymakers, people on a break from work. Even on a wet day an hour in a café watching Lord Street can be illuminating and rewarding. Elderly people walk slowly along arm in arm, seeing no need for the haste of people with only an hour away from their desk. Groups of young people are noisy and exuberant, wanting to be noticed, and mature couples spend time window shopping. But Lord Street is not as elegant as it was. The visitors are certainly not as smartly dressed, with training shoes and tracksuits replacing polished shoes and pressed skirts. Nikolaus Pevsner observed that many of Southport's visitors were not fashionable people, which is still true today. Fat visitors herd chubby, shaven children dribbling ice cream. They sit drinking beer from plastic glasses outside noisy bars, surrounded by fried chicken cartons, stomachs bulging under their football shirts, eyes hidden behind dark glasses. Litter is a problem here, as elsewhere, but on refuse collection days the shops have no alternative but to leave dozens of neat bin bags and taped cardboard boxes in front of the shops for the bin men.

The gigantic war memorial at the heart of Lord Street is not immune from this new mood. It is affectionately known as the Monument, and is a huge space open to wind and light and memory, designed for remembrance and contemplation. The Monument is surrounded by gardens, pools, trees, and occupies a whole town square; London Square was once a place for chair hire or tram rides, but it is now noisy and traffic-heavy, a place for meetings and drinking; it is always litter-blown, faintly greasy. The Monument seems oblivious. The solemn, classical architecture gives it an unassailable dignity, and with its large colonnades and obelisk, the Monument seems always to be obeying the two-minute silence, always remembering the dead, the wreaths at its foot in November like dribbles of spilled blood.

Lord Street seems quieter between the Monument and Manchester Road. There are

Municipal gardens and the town's bandstand. This area is popular with skateboarders and pensioners, which can lead to some friction.

Sunshine and shadows on the calm solemnity of the town's enormous war memorial.

fewer people and so the pavement seems wider, the street lamps more ornate and more obvious, and there seem far more trees. The whole street is defined by municipal landscaping, and even on this quieter stretch there are great concrete urns of flowers, grassy spaces and a small pool and fountain, rather old and mossy. It is near enough to Hesketh Park to attract ducks. This is the quieter end of Lord Street, perhaps the poorer end. The shops are not so glamorous here, and seem to cater for residents, not visitors.

The shopping arcades of Lord Street end at the large roundabout which connects Lord Street with Manchester Road. There is a great sense of space here, far greater at this end of Lord Street than at the other. The roundabout itself is graced with large flower beds and one of the elegant, almost Chinese, street lamps erected in 1953 to commemorate the Coronation. The approach roads seem wide and relatively quiet, and they are marked by four large and imposing buildings which seem well spaced in an open, flat landscape. The neat flourish of Tower Buildings, with its frothy ironwork and steep slated roof, echoes Pavilion Buildings at the Birkdale end. This is a landscape of towers, but Tower Buildings is dwarfed by the strong Sandown Court tower block across Leicester Road. It is not an attractive building, but the size and location make it imposing. To me it looks to date from the late 1950s or early 1960s, and its balcony boards and heavy lettering seem pure sunny west coast America, perhaps not out of place in a seaside town. There is a Chinese restaurant on the ground floor and even a fountain of dolphins at play, but it isn't often working. Buildings like these are rarer than they used to be but still common enough to be invisible. The magistrates' courts and fire station sit on the corner of Albert Road and Manchester Road and are unobtrusive and practical. They too are given grandeur by their location. The law courts have an impressive, almost Egyptian solemnity, with their blank walls and tall recessed columns framing the entrance staircase. It is an intimidating building even to relatively law-abiding citizens. The final corner of the roundabout is marked by the simple grace of Regent Court. This square tower block looks older than Sandown Court, and is a little more scruffy. It has a small supermarket on the ground floor instead of a restaurant, but the first floor is a well-hidden car park, and with its large overhanging roof the building is more attractive than its bigger neighbour. The little run of Manchester Road between here and Hoghton Street has some very attractive cottages in varying styles, well kept and neat, and an imposing terrace of Victorian or Edwardian town houses, five storeys of rather heavy ornament. Between them and the YMCA a new development of apartments is being built, the latest exercise in urban living.

But this landscape of tall buildings at the end of Lord Street is dominated by the magnificent tower of Holy Trinity Church, which stands on the corner of Manchester Road and Queen's Road/Hoghton Street. This is one of the landmarks of Southport,

Holy Trinity tower, one of the towers and spires of Lord Street which are visible for many miles.

both for its great height which makes it visible for miles and for its strange Gothic beauty; it looks like wet limestone has been dropped onto a plain brick tower then stretched and pulled like pizza cheese, until it ran down the building and cooled into gnarled fingers of stone. The mobile telephone equipment on the roof of Sandown Court is lumpy enough to echo the white pinnacles of Holy Trinity Church.

The grand boulevard of Lord Street ends here but the street line is carried on by Albert Road, which continues the straight line towards Hesketh Park. The houses start by being semi-detached or small detached houses, but get progressively grander the nearer they are to Hesketh Park. The Victorian styles are softened and Albert, Leyland, Alexandra and Saunders Roads have a pleasant mixture of houses with large gardens and some unusual landmarks; turrets and château towers on corners, tiny tower bedrooms. Perhaps they were thought pretentious at the time they were built, but now they add charm and character to these quiet streets with their view of the sand dunes towards the Promenade and Marine Drive. Hesketh Park is the most attractive green space in the town, and the roads around it have grand detached homes which look as though they were built at the end of the 19th century and through to the 1920s and 1930s. Some have retained their names, at least on gateposts if not in everyday use. 'Winterholme' is still carved onto a plaque in the wall, fading and crumbling, 'Sandal' is still deeply carved into the heavy gatepost of what is now a church. All the houses here have echoes of the sunshine styles of Italianate or Art Deco architecture, suggesting the light and airy nature of holiday and seaside life.

Tower buildings at the Churchtown end of Lord Street.

Hesketh Park. The carving used to line the path possibly came from the demolished All Saints' Church, and the glass house was photographed before the recent massive restoration project.

Lord Street defines Southport and has done so since the town's earliest days, when the first hotels and boarding houses were built in the sand dunes. It grew into a great boulevard, and along the way gave us one of Southport's most enduring if tongue-in-cheek stories. Legend has it that it was Lord Street that inspired Prince Louis Napoleon to redesign Paris as a city of great avenues with his architect, Baron Haussmann. So maybe the question should not be about this town, about Southport. Maybe the question should rather read: what would Paris look like without Lord Street?

Victorian dignity on Albert Road, Hesketh Park.

CHAPTER FIVE

TOWN STORIES

This is a collection of stories and histories that interested me about Southport, but which did not fit neatly into any of the other chapters. I wanted to write about the hidden landscapes around Lord Street, I was fascinated by the stories of the lost pleasure grounds of Kew and the Winter Gardens, and reading Cedric Greenwood and Rob Gell's excellent books on old railway stations made me curious about Southport's vanished railway landscapes. These were too small to have a chapter to themselves, but might have overbalanced another, bigger chapter.

Streetscapes

I have been interested for a long time in what urban writers call the 'streetscape' – the appearance and uses of town streets. From the air Southport looks like a fragment of an American town, a well-designed urban landscape curving in a great crescent, following the coastline as it broadly sweeps north-eastwards along the Ribble estuary. There are no hills, and the streets are long and straight, lined with Italianate houses; there are many white arches and heavy window frames, a lot of red brick. The skyline is made up of heavy tower blocks and church spires. I love this northern European quality to the town, the flat straight roads, the greenery, the red brick houses and old spires rising above the trees. Southport is centred on Lord Street and the Promenade, with a curving grid pattern of roads running out from the spine of Lord Street like ribs, meeting other roads at right angles. I believe that a town's life happens on its quiet streets, in its small warehouses and back street pubs, and around Lord Street and the Promenade is a hidden or invisible landscape of ordinary streets, some celebrated, some shamefully neglected and near derelict. Many have ornate buildings, invisible because

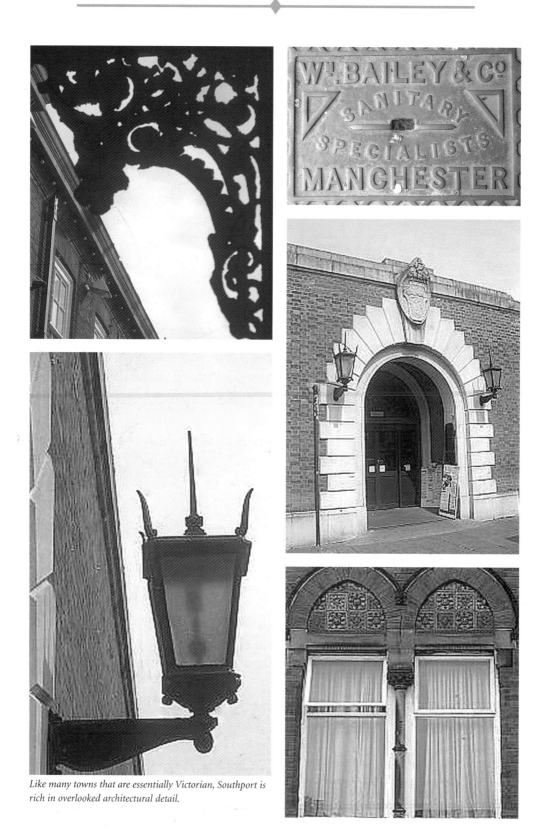

Like many towns that are essentially Victorian, Southport is rich in overlooked architectural detail.

Roofscapes and footscapes and plaques – it is worth wandering the streets simply to observe.

of traffic or crowded pavements; dazzling 1930s glass office blocks, solid commercial buildings with the towers and steep roofs of a French château, fading 1960s shop fronts. Southport is famous for this wealth of small shops and interesting back streets. Away from the bright lights there are family-run Italian restaurants and places to hire cake tins or buy replacement seals for obsolete machinery; discreet shops selling sophisticated lingerie, smart Chinese restaurants, spit and sawdust pubs. There are wine importers, curtain shops decorated with great lengths of fabric, a bookshop where new or second-hand purchases are still wrapped in brown paper and string and a fire always burns in the winter. One of the pleasures in exploring these overlooked landscapes lies in discovering the old and unusual in the surface of the streets that have survived for a century or more: Victorian manhole covers and drain covers, rusted ironwork that once supported a gate lamp or was just wrought for decoration, square blue floor tiles, granite kerb stones. In St Paul's Square, looking like a rather heavy, neglected street lamp, is 'J.E. Webb's Patent Sewer Gas Destructor'. It is covered now in layer upon layer of rusty paint, but it once burned off the sewer gases to light the streets, an example of Victorian practicality at its very best. There are a few of these around the town and a walk linking them would unearth many of the town's hidden sides. All over Southport there are little cobbled lanes leading to hidden courtyards; often they were old workshops or stable yards and have been taken over by small businesses such as paint shops and dealers in spare parts. These little alleyways and tiled yards are hidden from the main roads and their very ordinariness makes them invisible, but they give a poetic secrecy to the older parts of the town. And on this regular grid pattern of roads unexpected vistas appear; I am surprised to see landmarks such as the Marine Way Bridge or Holy Trinity church tower appear over the rooftops or at the end of long streets, making unlikely, exciting connections.

Nevill Street is a good example of a street full of overlooked stories. It runs from Lord Street to the Promenade and the modern Pier Pavilion, with its great carousel of painted horses. It is an ordinary town street yet it is endlessly fascinating for urban storytellers as beneath the tarmac are supposedly the remains of an older street; once the road from Lord Street ran to the sands under the Promenade, which leaped over Nevill Street on a solid bridge, enabling a row of shops to be built. This was one of the principal routes from the town centre to the beach, and it was lined with cafés and shops such as Ye Olde Castle Restaurant, the Southport Café and Gordon's Bazaar, to tempt the visitors. The Victoria Hotel had a luncheon bar and vaults in the Nevill Street subway, and opposite, beneath the baths, stood the premises of S. Broadbent, oyster merchant. They were here until 1903 when Nevill Street was raised to meet the Promenade, perhaps because of the increase in traffic. This place below the pavement, a world of smashed shop fronts boarded up and then buried, is an endless source of

SPENCER PLACE

Italianate splendour, Market Street.

regret and speculation; what survives down there? Is it possible to get in and see it? There are stories and rumours on Southport websites of lost entrances to old Nevill Street, of giant iron doors beneath the Pier Pavilion that somebody saw used as recently as the 1960s, giving access to this gloomy, destroyed world.

None of this can be seen today, and old Nevill Street can only be seen through stories and photographs in the town's archives. But modern Nevill Street is still an interesting mish-mash of the old and the new. Until recently a rather stern statue of Queen Victoria stood at the Promenade end, between the old Victoria Baths and the ugly flats built on the site of the Victoria Hotel. As part of the ongoing redevelopment of Nevill Street the old queen is moving again; she used to stand outside Cambridge Hall, and so is on a slow royal progress around the town. Perhaps future observers will see her on Lord Street again, or in Hesketh Park, or in a repository for old statues, like the corporation yards in India that are the final resting places for many of these reminders of the old empire. When I was a child, Southport seemed to me to still be a Victorian town, one untouched by the bombing of the war or the demolition of the 1960s, and I feel that the town should keep and enhance these connections with Victorian Britain; the town was largely created by the 19th century and is fortunate in having an almost intact Victorian heart. There is other, more subtle royalist celebration; behind Queen Victoria stands one of the elegant street lamps that the town's lighting committee erected in 1953 to celebrate the Coronation of Queen Elizabeth II.

Nevill Street also has Nevill Buildings, a grand Gothic building which seems out of place in restrained classical Southport, where only the churches seem Gothic. Giant lion and bear heads spout rainwater from deep gullies, and the building has smart pointed arch windows and steep gables. There is a peeling plaque erected by the British Film Institute to commemorate G.B. Samuelson, the film maker, who was born here.

Leo's Bar opposite has all the sunny exuberance of interwar design, simple clean lines and curving glass. There are a number of these sleek buildings hidden in Southport – the old Garrick Theatre, the McDonald's building on King Street, the Woolwich Building Society office on London Street. An interesting journey could be plotted between them, a walk through a recreated Southport of the interwar years. They are bright and cheerful buildings which have retained an optimistic, slightly retro modernity, even if they are unfashionable and a little unkempt today. Another side of seaside life between the wars can be seen on Bath Street, running off Nevill Street. Behind the grand façades of the Promenade are the boarding houses of seaside legend, the stuff of holiday fears and music hall jokes; intimidating places run by disapproving women with long lists of rules and regulations – no sand in the rooms, one egg for breakfast, no hot water after 6pm. Sadly modern guest houses and small hotels are no longer like this. They have minibars and satellite television and cater for the conference

The Town Hall steps and Cambridge Hall after a rare snowfall in around 1900. In bad light the monumental architecture has a great melancholy about it.

The shiny future – interwar architecture, London Street.

trade, which is increasingly important to the town, but I like to think that, in appearance at least, some of the older atmosphere has survived.

Ten minutes across Lord Street from Nevill Street takes us to Chapel Street. This seems to me a good example of a town centre road which is used badly; it is frenzied with traffic for most of the time, and one of the first sights a new visitor arriving by train sees is a wall of cars and buses. The traffic surging through seems clumsily handled, and walking here is difficult as the pavements are so busy and the road is so dominant. In a way Chapel Street is a victim of its own success. It has the town's major railway station and so brings people into Southport, but the street is too heavily congested to make the transport links feel simple and easy. There are shops and smart cafés, but it is not a glamorous street. Yet the buildings are elegant and attractive, with fine Dutch gables and modern Tudor frontages; and the BHS store, which is a fine wedding cake of a building, is rich with white plasterwork. Chapel Street sits at the heart of a small web of attractive, interesting streets and urban footpaths that run through the shops to the station or down ornate alleyways to reach Lord Street. Marble Place provides additional shops and is a new pedestrian street or arcade cut through the old urban fabric. Tulketh Street has the offices of the *Southport Visiter*, small shops and ample parking, and connects Chapel Street with the curious shops of Wesley Street. London Street is busy with traffic and shoppers but has some handsome buildings, neglected Victoriana, the town's most recent (and scandalous) lingerie shop and the best new-Irish pub in Southport. There are more shops on the Cambridge Arcade, although as it runs through to Lord Street it is often only used as a safe short cut. The arcade is one of the first things visitors see, but it is dirty and could be used with more imagination. Corporation Street runs through to the Town Hall, and has the beautiful Christ Church Higher Grade School building on it, a fantastic Moorish-Gothic concoction of carved stone and brickwork. But appreciating the architecture seems madness because of the traffic and people; for many years there have been plans to pedestrianise Chapel Street, to make it quieter and safer and allow the buildings to be appreciated and given new uses, but at the time of writing nothing has come of these ideas. With these connections to other places it should be a small town square, with pavement cafés, better signposts, perhaps a fountain or street sculpture. Ideally the buildings between here and Lord Street should be dynamited to make a large new square, a grand approach to the heart of the town. At the very least they should demolish the railway station; as the principal gateway to the town, but dirty and intimidating, it seems the least we deserve.

Chapel Street joins Eastbank Street at a busy but rather bleak junction, which used to have a large Congregational church on it, demolished some 40 years ago, and one long-gone entrance to the covered market. A shame, as this junction must have been very attractive then, and is still interesting now. The building society on the corner is a tall and richly decorated structure, with fiery red terracotta balustrades and urns high above the street. I have already mentioned the burger bar opposite, a striking interwar building with a great glass staircase shaft looming over the corner with King Street. Eastbank Street is one of the main roads of the town, connecting Scarisbrick New Road and the eastern suburbs with Lord Street. It is scruffy and many of the shops are run down or empty, yet here too there are attractive buildings. The street's three pubs are all housed in smart or unusual shells, the 1930s red brick of the Volunteer, the mosaics of the Ship and the snug domestic style of the Wellington, all sash windows and a roof of wide slates. The Volunteer stands on the corner of Wesley Street, which has reinvented itself as a commercial 'micro-village'. The shops here have banded together

The magnificent Viceroy Buildings, Eastbank Street.

A close-up of the Winter Gardens with a local 'mini-bus driver' and his assistant.

to advertise themselves jointly, to advertise the street rather than individual shops. Southport has a few of these enterprising micro-villages; Union Street, Scarisbrick Avenue and Birkdale Village spring to mind as having seen themselves in this new and imaginative way. Opposite the Volunteer stands the imposing Viceroy Buildings, presumably named after George Curzon, who was Southport's MP in the 1890s

The conservatory, Winter Gardens, c.1910.

before being made Viceroy of India. It is a gorgeous building of château turrets and steep red-tiled roofs, with imperial eagles and sandstone lions on the roofline. There are other echoes of India here; there are a number of Indian businesses on Eastbank Street and Viceroy Buildings stands opposite a smart Indian restaurant. This stands in a beautiful row of shops built as one long street front, and originally called something Buildings. But it is run down and neglected, and the name of the Buildings has been lost from the façade. The roofline is made up of a series of Dutch gables, and each of the handsome oriel windows has tiny eyes of stained glass which seem framed in a Moghul arch – to my eyes at least. One of the pleasures of idle street wandering is letting your mind make such romantic links.

Eastbank Street had the town's first railway station, but there is nothing to remind us of this today; no buildings survive and the tracks are lined with rubble and litter. Presumably the wooden 1840s station stood on a level crossing, but the road leaps over the railway today to end at the roundabout with a final flurry of shops under a simple

The Winter Gardens from King's Gardens. The pavilion is on the left and the giant glass roof of the conservatory is on the right.

glass awning. At the roundabout with Scarisbrick New Road and Shakespeare Street, the urban heart of Southport slips invisibly into a grey hinterland, streets of homes and shops that seem neither urban nor suburban. Many of the large Victorian houses on Talbot Street or Part Street for example are handsome and well-maintained, but others have been broken up into flats or bedsits, and the surrounding businesses are smaller. There are depots, small warehouses and builders' yards. Shakespeare Street has a fabulous array of shops, and sells everything from nails, drainpipes and vacuum cleaner

The Winter Gardens from the Promenade.

bags to three-piece suites, plaster Madonnas and 1920s brooches. It has good charity shops, Britain's only lawnmower museum and the Maze, a Royal Arcade for bargain hunters, a warren of old furniture, cookery books, paintings, china, glassware, road signs, 1930s lampshades. But here the urban heart seems to sputter to an end; the shops and small businesses finish, and the long streets run on into the suburbs.

Lost pleasure gardens

Every town has landscapes that are hidden from most visitors and perhaps most residents, and which survive now only in old photographs and archives, or in the names of streets. Southport has seen vast buildings come and go, some more interesting than others. On Lord Street stood the Glaciarium, where 'skating may be had on natural ice', and the Palais de Danse, which was a huge ballroom with high and ornate ceilings. But of all the great attractions of the town it was the Winter Gardens that fascinated me the most, perhaps because there seemed something official about this attraction, something municipal; it was *The* Winter Gardens or *Southport* Winter Gardens and, although Southport's were the first, today the name puts it on a par with other seaside resorts, seems to make it official. Yet, like many Victorian developments, the Gardens were built by a private business, the Southport Pavilion & Winter Gardens Company. It was private enterprise masquerading as civic philanthropy. Winter gardens were a Victorian idea, popular with seaside or holiday towns. Having a winter gardens seemed a part of Victorian civic pride, along with an art gallery, a town library and well-laid out parks. Perhaps they developed from the Georgian idea of assembly rooms, a place for socialising and town meetings, but their immediate inspiration was the Crystal Palace, built in 1851 for the Great Exhibition. New technology allowed the Victorians to create gardens unaffected by the weather, with promenading space and refreshment rooms, long galleries to converse in and admire the exotic or tender plants. Above all the technology allowed glass buildings of immense size to be built, and many seaside resorts had them; in a very different form, Blackpool's still exist. The idea has been recently revived by Sheffield, with a modern arched hall of tropical plants built in the city centre.

Southport's Winter Gardens, opened in 1874 and deliberately intended to rival the Crystal Palace in grandeur, stood between Coronation Walk and Lord Street railway station. They were perhaps the most lavish buildings ever erected in Southport, and comprised two large buildings, the conservatory and the concert pavilion, linked by a promenade. They dominated the skyline of the south Promenade, and the great glass roof of the conservatory dwarfed the tower of the railway station on Lord Street. Some guide books referred to the station as 'the Winter Gardens station' so close were the links between the Gardens and the railway building, which could after all bring thousands of visitors a day to the attractions next door. The giant glass roofs of the Winter Gardens would have been one of the first things seen as the visitors' trains approached the town, as everything was on a colossal scale. The iron and glass conservatory with its wealth of exotic plants was advertised as the largest in England, and the concert pavilion could seat 2,500 people; at its height a 30-piece orchestra gave two performances a day. Beneath the promenade were refreshment rooms and a large aquarium, big enough to become a zoo later on. 'The chief and central attraction of Southport is certainly to be found in its far-famed Winter Gardens,' wrote a guide to the town in 1889. 'This magnificent institution covers an immense area of ground and combines within itself a most infinite variety of attractions and amusements.' In 1891 the Winter Gardens opened an opera house on the site, a fantastic building designed by Frank Matcham, the foremost theatre architect of his day.

But Southport could not sustain such a vast and expensive complex of buildings, and the Winter Gardens were not a commercial success. The grand Opera House burned down in 1929. The great glass house was taller and longer than the central section of the Kew Palm House, but the taste for admiring exotic plants had passed and it was converted for more mundane uses, first to a ballroom and later for rollerskating. The building was demolished in 1933, but perhaps there are still elderly Southport residents who remember dancing in the Conservatory of the Winter Gardens. More people will remember the Pavilion, which survived another 30 years as a cinema and theatre and came down in 1962.

Nothing survives today of the Winter Gardens. Even the pattern of roads has changed in this landscape, as if the magnetic power of a great building has been released and the roads have moved. The landscaping has been concreted over, and car parks and bin bays now occupy the site. The railway lines that ran out towards the sea and then swept around to follow the coastline are gone. Kingsway now connects the Promenade with Lord Street over the Winter Gardens, and a large supermarket occupies part of the site and the rear of the old railway station. Yet is it too fanciful to see here a deliberate architectural echo, a conscious choice by the architect to remember

Alexandria Gardens (left) and Kew Gardens (right).

the Winter Gardens? Modern technology has allowed a light, airy roofline of glass pyramids and white struts that seem an echo of spindly ironwork. Lightweight tubular steel recalls ironwork, domes, glass rooflines, railway architecture and greenhouses, a blurring of design and purpose that would have pleased the Victorians. And, suitably enough for a modern grocery store, the building

One of the woodland walks, Kew Gardens.

also resembles one of the great Victorian public markets. From Lord Street the view through the portico of the old railway station is a blur of stonework, pathways, ironwork and glass, lacking only greenery to give an echo of the structures that once stood here.

The Winter Gardens are not the only lost pleasure gardens in Southport. Of all the landscapes that I wanted to explore and write about, Kew seemed to me to be one of the oddest. I had always known that the district was named after Kew Gardens, but where were they? And the name, the magical arrogance of the name. Kew is an area of eastern Southport which seems centred on a roundabout and a business park, a landscape built for motor cars and shopping, not a landscape of plants and flowers, pathways and promenades. But in the 1860s a large garden landscape was laid out between Boundary Brook and Town Lane, in a broad triangle along Scarisbrick New Road. They were named Alexandra (not Alexandria) Gardens to begin with and only became Kew Gardens much later. The Gardens were a success to begin with and from the early 1880s a tram service ran from London Square down Scarisbrick New Road, which was then still quite rural, to the Richmond Hotel at the entrance to the Gardens.

They were successful enough to add a zoo later on, and there were illuminated carnivals on the lake. A visitor in 1889 wrote of the attractions that were on offer:

An hotel, a magnificent pavilion capable of affording shelter to about one thousand persons, extensive

The Zoo Gardens at Kew.

tea and other refreshment rooms, large conservatories and other ornamental plant and fruit houses, a beautiful lake for boating and skating, extending over two acres, tastefully diversified with islands and bridges, and having a choice profusion of boats for the use of visitors, with bowling greens, tennis lawns, and swings, with elaborate and well-laid-out grounds of over thirteen acres charmingly varied by hill and dale, promontories and recesses with the most graceful curves and undulating lines, not only beautiful in themselves but affording protection to a splendid collection of the more rare and otherwise tender plants. The walks are varied and numerous, embracing every point of interest and beauty, now on the summit of a hill, or meandering through rocks and ferns, or passing through gorgeous flower gardens, imposing avenues, lovely nooks and corners, rocky arches, cosy seats and summer houses for rest and shelter, with a thousand other attractions that would carry us beyond our limits to describe, the whole forming an attraction for the visitor to Southport such as once seen will not readily be forgotten.

Even allowing for Victorian hyperbole, Kew Gardens must have been an astonishing sight, surrounded as they were by fields and farmland. Surviving pictures show long straight avenues through the woods, huge flower beds, classical urns full of flowers, large statues, distant glasshouses and towers not dissimilar to the Winter Gardens. There was even a Kew Gardens railway station, on the Altcar Bob line to Halsall and Barton, which stood on what is now Foul Lane and Kew Business Park. The station was on a high level to allow the railway to cross Scarisbrick Road on a bridge.

But even today this district is on the outskirts of Southport. On the Ordnance Survey map of 1911 the neat Gardens are surrounded by fields and coverts, and Town Lane runs through open countryside. Perhaps it was just too far out from the town centre for visitors. The tram route was closed in 1916, and the Gardens began to decline. They closed in the early 1920s and reopened in 1928, but the new opening was not a success and Kew Gardens closed for good in the early 1930s. Judging by the age of the houses on Scarisbrick New Road, the land began to be sold off almost immediately for new housing. Some of the landscaping survived for a time behind the houses, and this patch of dense woodland is now called Kew Woods. Most of the grounds disappeared 30 or 40 years ago, with the building of the Queenscourt Hospice and the new hospital, but enough survived in the 1960s to be an unofficial playground for children from King George V school.

There is a new tarmac path from Town Lane, Kew, to Scarisbrick New Road, which marks roughly the western boundary of the Gardens. It is difficult to say now what is old and what is not, as with the building of the two medical facilities from the 1960s onwards, roads were realigned and boundaries became confused. I had hoped to find balustrades half buried in the woods, a toppled urn too heavy to move or overgrown pathways, but nothing survives today of the 13 acres, the hills, the flower beds. The woods are very dense and fenced off with three or four lines of heavy wire, but few of the trees look old enough to remember the Gardens. The new path skirts hospital car parks and a small lake, now reserved for the Kew Anglers. Was this part of the two-acre lake with the islands and ornamental bridges? It is difficult to say. The impenetrable woods are more like a nature reserve than a park, perhaps intentionally. Any surviving features of the old Kew Gardens are now well buried. The path emerges at the north-western boundary of the Gardens, the Boundary Brook, onto the busy Scarisbrick New Road. The only other reminder of Kew Gardens is the Richmond Hotel. This too is a disappointment, as it is a modern replacement of the old Alexandra Hotel, no more than 20 years old, and it holds no memories; images of the Gardens are rare and there are no pictures or maps on the pub walls. To the rear of the pub is a low wall of dressed stones that I like to think were found in the ruins and reused. Most impressively there are trees here which seem old enough to have been saplings 80-odd years ago, and one giant in particular which could have stood here when the trams turned around outside the Alexandra Hotel, at the entrance to Kew Gardens. But distances do not change, and I found myself walking the same few hundred yards along Scarisbrick New Road to the junction with Town Lane that weary garden visitors walked on their way to the railway station. Across the endless streams of traffic and the modern landscaping are the ugly sheds of the business park, where the station used to be. Few landscapes in Southport have changed as much as this in the last century.

Forgotten railway stations

One of my earliest Southport memories is of a chips-and-egg-sandwiches picnic on Lord Street, when I was part of a group of teenage railway enthusiasts celebrating the end of our exams by visiting Steamport. I was always more interested in derelict station buildings than the steam engines or the rolling stock, and abandoned or forgotten railway stations were an especial love of mine. There seems particular poignancy about a lost railway station; perhaps we mourn Victorian faith in technological progress and private enterprise, or simply look back to a railway system that seemed to work. The sheer weight and solidity of railway stations and railway lines makes it astonishing to think that they could vanish, but they do, even from memory. Photographs of old stations seem always to have been taken in the summer, with a peculiar black-and-white conjuring of hot afternoons, the hiss of steam, the feel of warm wood. They have the same sadness as a black-and-white film, and colour pictures or those featuring diesel or electric trains seem already to be rushing towards the closures and demolition of the Beeching Plan, when so many stations were lost. The names of lost railway stations conjure a world familiar yet remote, and suggest journeys which are no longer possible, a landscape which has disappeared. This strange world of real places connected by long-gone rails has all the poignancy of a failed love affair.

I have stolen the title of this piece from Cedric Greenwood, who wrote that Southport had 22 railway stations, 16 of which were in use simultaneously. This astonishing number has been whittled down considerably over the last 40 years or so, and the modern town has many lost stations. Churchtown once had a railway station, on the line to Hesketh Park and Crossens. Blowick's station stood near the Thatch and Thistle pub, and nearby Butts Lane had a small halt. The Palace Hotel in Birkdale was important enough to have a railway station of its own, as was Kew Gardens. Places not

Southport's first railway station? The Liverpool, Crosby & Southport railway building on Portland Street.

Southport rails from the air – from the left, Chapel Street Station and the engine shed and passenger terminal of Central Station.

seemingly big enough to have a station also had them: Ash Street, St Luke's, Ainsdale Beach. Some are only empty and disused, but most have disappeared completely and only exist in old photographs and the threads of local history websites. The lines ran at

various times from a number of town centre stations – Southport Central, Southport Lord Street, Southport Chapel Street – out to Liverpool, Manchester, Wigan and Preston. The history of these railway lines reflects the importance of the holiday and commuter traffic to the railway companies, as a large number of them vied for the passengers. Their names have all the passion and urgency of the Victorian railway age, the excitement of connecting small towns to each other by rail: the West Lancashire Railway, the St Helens & Southport

Sunlight on the clean stonework of Lord Street Station.

Railway, the Manchester, Wigan & Southport Railway, the East Lancashire Railway. The first to reach Southport was the Liverpool, Crosby & Southport Railway, whose line through Crosby is still the connection to Liverpool. Two of their buildings survive, on the level crossings at Duke Street and Portland Street. These modest and rather battered buildings look like old crossing keepers' cottages, but the one at Portland Street was definitely part of Southport's first station, and has stood next to the railway line since 1848.

Lord Street station is still standing, and the fine tower is one of the first landmarks on Lord Street seen by road traffic arriving from Liverpool. The station was built by the grandly named Southport & Cheshire Lines Extension Railway, and opened in 1884. This must have been one of the best ways to arrive in the town. The line ran in a roundabout way from Liverpool through Woodvale, Ainsdale Beach and the station for the Birkdale Palace Hotel, to enter Southport in a dramatic sweep and terminate on Lord Street. From the high station at Woodvale the sand dunes and pine woods must have appeared, then glimpses of the sea; finally Southport's towers rising over the sandy hills must have meant the end of the journey, and the start of the holiday. The last train ran into Lord Street in 1952, and the stations at Birkdale Palace and Woodvale are long gone. Much of the trackbed was reused in the 1960s as the coast road, and the railway station at Ainsdale Beach has been turned into a pub.

There were other, less dramatic stations in the town centre. London Street station was built by the East Lancashire company and the giant Lancashire & Yorkshire Railway, and stood next to Chapel Street station. It disappeared when that station was expanded in 1914. The Steamport preservation group occupied the engine shed of the old Southport Central Station on Derby Road, a quiet unobtrusive building behind what I remember as a coal yard and a weighbridge, a place of lorries. I remember that Steamport always seemed deserted and the long train shed was strangely silent for all the lines of dismantled trams and engines. Southport Central was the terminus of the West Lancashire Railway from 1882, and the trains ran from here to Preston. The Liverpool, Southport & Preston Junction Railway also ran trains to Halsall and Altcar, the Altcar Bob line, out of Central Station from 1887. The Lancashire & Yorkshire Railway absorbed these small companies in 1897 and closed Central in 1901. It was used as a freight terminal until the 1970s, and I have an older, vaguer memory of the grand but rather lumpy station building on the corner of Kensington Road, even then boarded up and inaccessible. These station buildings have now all gone and the site is occupied by the vast Centre 12 shopping development; shops and a huge car park stand on the site of the railway lines.

Where there are closed railway stations there is usually a closed railway line, but their courses can still be traced and there is great pleasure to be had from sketching the

Chapel Street Station just after World War One. This was replaced in the early 1920s by the ugly station of today.

course of a line onto a modern map. The curves are smooth and the route seems inevitable. In open country they have often been reused as cycle paths or walking routes and are often marked 'dismantled railway' but even on town plans their route can be seen; a strange gap between streets, a bridge for no reason, a new straight road that takes advantage of the old trackbed. From Central Station the railway led to St Luke's and Ash Street stations, on St Luke's Road. St Luke's opened in 1883 to take passengers out to Wigan and Preston, but new housing occupies what was once station platforms and cinder track. Ash Street station stood next door, on the curve of track heading for Meols Cop; this opened in 1878 as Southport Windsor Street and was the terminus of the West Lancashire Railway until 1882. The road is busy and it is difficult to see over the wall, but in any case nothing survives of either station. From here one line ran under Hawkshead Street and through what are now the grounds of the Holy Family Primary School, to the station at Hesketh Park. This stood opposite Preston Road on Park Avenue. From Hesketh Park it ran to Churchtown, from there to Crossens, and then out across farmland to Hesketh Bank, and eventually Preston. This was known as the Celery Line, because of the market gardens it served. (I am so used to hearing of railway lines being closed that it startled me to realise that on many railway lines all the stations would have opened on the same day, from one end of the line to the other.) From St Luke's another line ran dead straight between Forest Road and Hart Street, where on modern maps the roads are disjointed still, to Blowick station. This stood on a level crossing on Meols Cop Road before the line ran to Pool Hey Junction, where it joined the line from Meols Cop station that still connects the town with Wigan.

The famous Altcar Bob line passed near Blowick on its way out from Central station to Hillhouse and Altcar. This railway is still remembered with affection in the town, and is one of the routes mentioned whenever the idea of improving rail connections is discussed. From Meols Cop and a small halt on Butts Lane, the tiny Altcar Bob trains went through Kew Gardens Station and over the Scarisbrick Road on the Kew Embankment, which can still be seen from the car park of the giant superstore. This long incline lead to a tiny station at Heathey Lane, just a flight of steps under the road bridge. From there it passed through a proper station at Shirdley Hill and another tiny halt at New Cut Lane to Halsall, Plex Moss Lane and Barton/Downholland, before joining the Cheshire Lines at Hillhouse Junction. The line closed to great regret in 1938, and very little survives of any of these stations, although the green scars and low embankments across the fields can still be seen. The small halts at Heathey Lane and New Cut Lane have disappeared, although the fine bridges are still standing, still smudged with soot from the last trains to use the line over 40 years ago. The station buildings have gone from Shirdley Hill, where a small plaque records the line's history, and a housing estate has been built in its place. The station at Halsall is now a private house, but the platforms at Barton/Downholland were still visible as recently as the 1980s.

Southport now has only one main station. Chapel Street was originally built in 1851 as the terminus of the Liverpool, Crosby & Southport Railway. The station at Portland Street/Eastbank Street had only been open two years, but already it was too small and too far out of the town. As the Lancashire & Yorkshire swallowed its competitors, Chapel Street became Southport's central railway station, and old photographs show a classical building with a large iron porch over the road to allow passengers to leave their cabs without getting wet. This elegant but muted building was deemed unsafe in 1970/71, and was replaced by the modern concourse. Arriving in Southport by train today is a dismal experience. The trains clatter in from Liverpool or Wigan and terminate at a huge glass and iron warehouse, seemingly too big for the traffic it takes. The station is uninviting and claustrophobic, built of concrete and grimy white mosaic tiles. The route out to Chapel Street is crowded and oppressive, with people silhouetted against the daylight and the directions confusing. It is dirty and noisy and very badly signposted. Chapel Street station is a poor introduction to a place that sees itself as a garden city, a place of elegant buildings, long vistas and promenades; but it is the only station to be demolished and completely rebuilt, so perhaps one of Southport's greatest lost stations is still here.

CHAPTER SIX

URBAN VILLAGES

In its 200-year history, Southport has grown from a small holiday resort to a modern town stretching from Marshside to Woodvale. It has absorbed many smaller villages in this growth, and in the evolution of North Meols into 'Southport and district', many of these places lost all individuality. Crossens and Blowick are now just suburbs of Southport, when a century ago they were small rural villages. Ainsdale has been absorbed by the municipal reality of Southport, but it has a heart of its own and is separated from Southport by a green belt, albeit a narrow strip of cemeteries, and so does not feel to me to be a part of the town. On the other hand new civic boundaries and suburbanisation did not destroy the identities of Birkdale and Churchtown. Both managed to keep a sense of their own identity, and survive within the patchwork of Southport as urban villages.

Birkdale

There is no longer a geographical border between Southport and Birkdale. Cedric Greenwood saw lines on street maps marking the old borders between mediaeval manors, roads that stopped abruptly, the uneven lines that defined garden boundaries; but in everyday use these are meaningless. There are few differences in the architecture, no new street signs, and a casual visitor would not know that he had passed from one into the other. But Birkdale has a very different mood to Southport, and an identity of its own. It feels quiet, almost drowsy, and is obviously a residential district, a suburb. It was a separate town until 1912, when it became part of Southport, and the loss of the Town Hall and Carnegie Library in the 1960s is still mildly resented. It is a town for older people, and I imagine that local teenagers spend their free time in Southport

Ironwork and stonework in Birkdale village.

rather than Birkdale. The charm of the place is not apparent to younger people, who generally have no interest in gardens or fascinating architecture. I like Birkdale. I like the contrast between the big houses of Birkdale Park and the smaller houses of Birkdale Common, what a friend calls Birkdale and Bairkdale, mimicking the Liverpool voices heard there. I like this sense of everyday history in Birkdale, this layering of people and place, of shifting populations and new towns. The truth is that Liverpool voices can be heard all over here, even in the huge houses near the shore and the golf courses. This part of Birkdale was built for the motor car and makes for long walking, but the huge 1930s houses on Waterloo Road still have an attractive holiday frivolity to them for all their size. The best are whitewashed and still defiantly modern after 70-odd years – the Round House, the White House, the clock tower of Hillside Golf Club – with expensive views across the sand dunes to the coast and the distant Welsh hills. The roads behind Waterloo Road are less interesting and more security-conscious; even bricklayers look at passers-by with suspicion. This is wealthy Birkdale, a wary suburb of security gates, expensive cars, intercoms. For all their landscaping and big gardens, these roads are cold and intimidating, and I prefer the older, warmer streets nearer the village centre. Many of the tall, confident Victorian houses on Weld Road and the surrounding roads have been turned into flats or nursing homes. Some stand empty and derelict, with

Interesting architecture and leafy streets – Birkdale village in the early morning.

A winter's dusk at Birkdale railway station – now the only station serving Birkdale but still largely as the Lancashire & Yorkshire Railway built it.

In its attractive architecture and glass awnings, Birkdale village has deliberate echoes of Lord Street.

their paint peeling and doors boarded up, grass growing like unkempt hair over stone paths and edging. It is a good area and they are largely safe from vandalism, but their stained glass windows let light into dusty unused halls.

Birkdale suffers from the gin-and-tonic, golf club image, but in reality it is a mixed suburb with residents working in central Southport or Liverpool, who are by no means all retired or fabulously wealthy. There are poorer streets and streets with cramped and awkward housing, too small in many cases for the families that live there; their possessions spill out into the gardens. The streets away from the shore are generally quiet and the semi-detached houses are attractive, built from the 1850s in a deliberate series of 'estates' and sharing many architectural features; they are mostly built of warm red brick, with slate roofs and gardens front and back. I like the streetscape, the way the roads look, in this quieter, cheaper Birkdale. Many of the pavements are still made of Victorian red-blue tiles, each one seemingly unique, with the footprints of small animals and birds and the badges of manufacturers pressed into them. Some have the mysterious letter E, perhaps to indicate the electricity supply. The mason's marks and symbols carved into the sandstone kerbstones are still readable despite a century of weathering, and the chequer-board manhole covers have BDC or BLB on them still, showing that they were put down by the Birkdale Local Board or Birkdale District Council, both abolished nearly 100 years ago. Sometimes these streets have the old street lamps, perhaps converted from gas but still with their unusual Gothic bases.

Victorian villas and an interesting roofline – Alma Road, Birkdale.

Birkdale has retained an identity independent of Southport because of Birkdale village, the shops and restaurants at its very heart, without which the town's identity would have disappeared. There are a number of 'urban villages' on this coast, starting perhaps with Waterloo then Crosby, Formby, Ainsdale and Birkdale; these have avoided blurring into one large dormitory town along the railway line, and have all managed to retain a unique identity. Modern Birkdale village has grown around the railway station, built by the Lancashire & Yorkshire Railway in 1851 and still in good condition. As it was built to serve the wealthy residents of Birkdale Park it is an elegant railway station, and now the most ornate on the line, with handsome glass and ironwork, and the original wooden hand rails, awnings and brick. The old stationmaster's house still stands next door. Birkdale is smarter than Southport but works hard to keep its 'urban village' atmosphere. The architecture in the village is interesting and eclectic, making an attractive streetscape linked by glass-and-iron awnings similar to those on Lord Street, and in similarly varying states of repair. The broad pavements have mature trees and are wide enough for tables and chairs in the summer. The shops fight hard against the vicious competition from the supermarkets and remind me of shops in an upmarket London suburb, the archetypal urban village. There are two fashionable wine bars, two smart interior design stores, a large wine warehouse, the best cheese shop in old Lancashire and a big, cheerful pub. There are places to eat and drink, buy clothes, buy children's shoes; the fishmongers' shop has a game licence and in the winter months sells teal, snipe and mallard shot on the fields behind the village.

In a town with an older population history is lightly buried, like driftwood covered with a gritty layer of sand. There are plenty of people who still remember the older elements of Birkdale, the Town Hall, the Carnegie Library, the Palace Hotel, all lost in the late 1960s when it must have felt that everything of any interest was being demolished. I was intrigued by the references to a Palace; there is a Palace development company and a Palace Road, and I wondered if perhaps Birkdale had a Palace the way Wigan had a Pier. But it is a true story. The Palace Hotel stood parallel to modern Palace Road on Weld Road, and when it opened in 1866 was the most fashionable hotel in the neighbourhood, and possibly one of the finest hotels in the country. It was a gigantic building, a Southport landmark, and the sheer scale of the building is difficult to imagine today. It was six storeys high, 17 bays long and had 1,000 rooms, with suites of spacious and lofty bedrooms, marble and granite baths, and a recreation room big enough to hold 500 people. The dining hall could seat 150 people at a time, and an 1889 guide commented that 'the cuisine and cellars of the Palace are a fit subject for the praise of the most fastidious gastronome.' It was big enough to have its own railway station, and later ran an air service to Blackpool from the hard flat Birkdale sands. What was it like, this vast building? What were the rooms like, what did the corridors feel like?

It was an imposing building but not an attractive one, and photographs show an odd cross between a château and a prison, rising above the dunes like a casino-hotel on the Belgian coast; it looks dark to me, but the views across the sand dunes and out to sea must have been superb. Unusual buildings attract strange stories, and there is a gloomy atmosphere surrounding this building: ghost stories, tragedies, disasters. Sometimes even research stories slip through your fingers. I found a website of personal reminiscences of holidays in Birkdale, with photographs from the 1950s of a Humber car on the beach for a family picnic and the sombre mass of the Palace Hotel rising behind it, but looking again the website had disappeared and I could not find the images a second time.

The strange stories of the Palace range from the comic to the tragic and heroic. It was long rumoured that the hotel was built the wrong way round, and that when he realised this the architect committed suicide by jumping from the roof. But it makes perfect sense to me to have the entrance facing away from the strong sea winds and the rain, and this attempt to contain the monster building sounds like a local joke. And I have read that the architect went on to design other buildings, but gruesome stories have a way of sticking and the stories of the Palace have become part of the folklore of Southport.

And perhaps the stories stick because the Palace was not a success. The local writer and journalist Peter Elson suggested recently that the hotel was something of a white elephant, suffering from an unsatisfactory location. Despite having hotels, the beach and even the Esplanade, Birkdale never rivalled Southport as a holiday destination and perhaps the Palace was too far from the bright lights, despite its railway station and landing strip. Financing such a giant proved ruinous, and in 1881 the Palace was reconstructed as a hydropathic hotel, that mixture of holiday-and-health cure that seems peculiarly Victorian. Others in Southport had been immediately successful and one still survives; the Smedley Hydropathic Establishment on the corner of Grosvenor Road and Trafalgar Road is now used as government offices but the grand rooms are intact.

The Palace Hotel was big enough to be involved in much of Southport's history. The coroner's court for the *Mexico* disaster was held here in December 1886, while the bodies of the lost lifeboat crews were laid out in the coach house next door, a tragedy that still resonates in Southport. The Palace was a great success as a rest home for wounded American military personnel during World War Two, as the size allowed entire bomber crews to convalesce together, and in all some 15,000 soldiers recuperated here – an astonishing number. A search for 'Birkdale Palace' on the Internet will reveal some of their stories of everyday kindnesses, taking tea with local people and dancing with Southport girls, the wartime memories of elderly soldiers from Wyoming or

Minnesota. The Palace was famous for its entertainment and dances after the war, but seems rarely to have been full of paying guests. In 1961 a small girl was murdered in the hotel, a crime which shocked Southport and ruined its image as a place where such things didn't happen. Peter Elson believes that the murder shattered any chances the hotel had of survival. In February 1967 there were only two residents in the 1,000-room hotel, and it closed forever later that year.

After closure, the Palace had a sad half-life as a film set. Boris Karloff filmed here possibly twice, working on *The Sorcerers* and *The Crimson Altar*. Norman Wisdom filmed some of *What's Good for the Goose* in the building, and the Dennis Price film *The Dark* was shot in the cellars. Perhaps from scene-by-scene examination and cross-cutting of these and other obscure films a purely architectural film could be created, clumsy footage of various rooms in the Palace at the end of the 1960s. But such a huge

building could not be sustained by this meagre work and in 1969, despite local opposition, the Birkdale Palace was demolished. Even then the building generated sad ghost stories of eerie noises in the corridors, lifts that moved without electricity, strange voices coming from empty rooms.

This is another of Southport's landscapes which has changed

The Mexico, *washed up on Birkdale Sands, December 1886.*

dramatically in 40 years. The estate of clean seaside houses on Palace Road was built over the old trackbed and railway station for the hotel, and there are houses too where the tennis courts stood, over the driveways and gardens, and where the six storeys of the hotel rose into the sky. From the photographs there seems to have been a great sense of open space about this landscape until the late 1960s. The big Victorian houses here stood in their own grounds, and the Palace grounds ran from Westcliffe Road across Palace Road to the railway line and the open dunes. When the Palace was demolished and the new houses were built, the area sank into ordinary suburbia and today even the street pattern is different, as if the magnetic influence of the giant building died with it and freed the roads to follow other patterns. A tide of 1970s houses has covered the site, submerging all references or markings, as if the Palace had never been: plate glass and stone cladding, pine trees and shaved grass.

But not all of the vast hotel was demolished. The Fishermen's Rest pub on Weld Road was once the coach house for the hotel, but by the late 1960s it had been converted into a non-residents' bar, and so was saved from the general demolition. Here is more layering of history: in the old public bar of the hotel I was able to sit and read what few stories I could find about the Palace. I find the stories and the history of the old hotel strangely moving, this mixture of Victorian confidence, failure, tragedy, murder and farce. The Fishermen's Rest at lunchtime is a cheerful, bustling pub, smelling of chip grease; it is loud with laughter, the thump of pop music and the clatter of dishes, a modern retro-Victorian pub in the shell of a 19th-century bar, with modern engraved glass and pub paraphernalia. It has the high ceilings of a far bigger building and there are pictures of the Palace from the air, but only one aspect of the hotel's story is really remembered; the Fishermen's Rest is a shrine to the two lifeboat crews lost in the *Mexico* disaster in 1886, whose bodies were once laid out in this room. Southport is still haunted by the memory of the *Mexico*. The ship ran into a sandbank in a storm in December 1886, and 14 men from the Southport lifeboat *Eliza Fernley* and the entire crew of the St Anne's lifeboat *Laura Janet* lost their lives in answering the distress call. The wreck of the *Mexico* is still one of the worst disasters in the history of the RNLI. Washed ashore on Birkdale Sands, the bodies of the dead lifeboatmen were brought to the Palace Hotel and laid out side by side for identification, while the hastily convened coroner's court was also held in the building. And on every 9 December at 10pm, the hour when the distress call was heard, the Fishermen's Rest falls quiet and is called to order for the toast: 'To the coxes and crews who died'.

The modern pub has Victorian conservatory planting, nautical carving and the polished brass of tiny ships' wheels. There are photographs of sepia boats against vast grey skies; the skies are still there through the opaque windows, past the modern houses and the road signs. There is a collecting box for the RNLI on a shelf, and photographs of Henry Robinson and John Jackson, the two Southport lifeboatmen who survived. They were photographed days or weeks later, dignified uncomfortable Victorians with moustaches and heavy water gear; one too of Henry Robinson in later life, a nervous, portly man outside a terraced house. The 14 mermaid brackets holding the rail to the bar commemorate the dead; and yet 'time' is rung on a 'Titanic 1912' bell, as if to link this disaster to other maritime tragedies, and the greatest of them all in the public imagination. Or perhaps we are being told to not dwell too much on the *Mexico*, that there were other disasters, worse disasters, that the sea had taken before and will take again. A plaque outside the pub recalls the dead lifeboatmen in verse; it is a sentimental poem yet strangely moving, and I was reminded of the monument to the *Mexico* dead in Duke Street Cemetery, a solid block of frozen granite violence. History is layered here – as I walked away from the Fishermen's Rest I could hear a voice calling for the Searchers on the juke box.

The Sefton coast is littered with shipwrecks and records of violent storms. In his book *The Battle of Land and Sea*, William Ashton wrote a list of small settlements –

The Park public house, Birkdale.

farms, hamlets and villages – that have been lost to the sea along this coast over the centuries. There is a harsh Norse poetry in even a selection of these ancient names; Meandale, Gripnottes, Anoldisdall, Winscarth-lithe, Quitemeledale, Halsteadhow. Birkdale once had an older relative, a Norse village called Argar Meols, which was supposedly far nearer the sea. The village was mentioned in the Domesday Book, although part of the village also seems to have been 'Birkedale' in around 1200. It was perhaps a fishing village in the relatively stable ground between the sea and the marshland behind the dunes, especially as for centuries the hard flat beach was used as a roadway between coastal settlements. This coast has always been used by fishermen, and there are still the boats and vehicles of cocklers and shrimpers on the coast at Birkdale Sands today. Argar Meols was swept away by a violent sea storm in the late Middle Ages; some say 1400 as a date, others say the 16th century. Nothing survives of it today, and the survivors did not write down their experiences for posterity. The village disappeared; modern Birkdale is now hidden from the sea behind a range of sand dunes, and Weld Road connects the village with the sea, as straight as the flight of an arrow; but where was Argar Meols? Was the sea nearer then, six centuries ago? Or are the large houses and flats built over the mediaeval village? The sand dunes here are high and full of rabbits, even near the traffic. On clear days there are good views of

Blackpool over the muddy estuary of the Ribble, a distant glimpse of towers and whitewashed buildings. The sea's calm is deceptive, and walking the beach trails in the evening I have sometimes wondered if the turf-and-cobble streets of sea-rotted Argar Meols are there under the sand.

It would appear that any survivors of the storm moved further inland to Birkdale, as Argar Meols does not seem to have been rebuilt. It is probable that this older Birkdale village was a small settlement on Birkdale Common, perhaps at a meeting point of Churchgate and the road across the Common towards Scarisbrick, in modern terms somewhere on Liverpool Road near the junction with Shaftesbury Road. This was a landscape of high sandy dune/hills on the edge of Birkdale Moss. The soil was poor and mostly sand, which even today lies just beneath the surface, and the fields would have been vulnerable to wind-blown sand despite the hills. These great mounds of sand were a feature of this coast until well into the 20th century, and it was observed at the end of the Victorian age that Birkdale was divided into the 'hawes' and the 'heys', the sand hills and the fields. Nothing of this older Birkdale village survives, but there were still ancient farm buildings here at the beginning of the 20th century, and even today there are older houses at the Liverpool Road/Shaftesbury Road junction, buildings smaller than the surrounding houses; they do not seem to be ancient cruck-built cottages but are

The oldest building in modern Birkdale, the thatched cottage on Liverpool Road.

perhaps isolated brick farm buildings. They are surrounded now by the familiar streets of the modern red-brick village.

Churchgate

In the mid-19th century the scattered village of Birkdale began to be transformed into a suburban village, and many of the old lanes and farm tracks – some probably hundreds of years old – were written over by the new roads. But I was fascinated to discover that Southport has remembered one of these old roads – Kirkgate or Churchgate, which possibly ran from the ancient church at Sefton to St Cuthbert's Church in Churchtown, and further north to link the scattered communities along the Ribble shoreline with the church. This is one of the most poetic lost roads in Lancashire. The legend has it that St Cuthbert's bones rested here during their long journey around northern England during the time of the Norse raids in the 10th century, so it is possible that Churchgate is 1,000 years old. The journey of St Cuthbert's bones is remembered in a string of places across the country, and locally there are also churches in Lytham and Halsall dedicated to him. How long the saint's bones stayed here is not known, but perhaps Churchgate began as a trail on solid ground between the sand dunes and the Moss to the saint's body, or perhaps this solid ground was already an established trail, and only later came to be given the name Churchgate, a Norse name. History is full of quirks and it is ironic that the only name we have for this ancient route is the one given it by the Norse invaders.

The Victorian photographer Henry Sampson took this photograph of Churchgate in 1860. This part of the old road was often called Snuttering Lane and is now Cemetery Road.

Churchgate was a highly important road, the only route to Churchtown, and for centuries Birkdale families used the road to attend church at St Cuthbert's. When a death occurred in Birkdale the coffin was carried all the way along the Churchgate to the church, although the cortège traditionally stopped at the Birkdale boundary and laid the coffin on a large boulder while the bearers rested their limbs. The boulder, which also served as a boundary stone, had a hollow where rainwater collected and it was the custom to sprinkle the coffin with water from this hollow. This odd practice may record a folk memory of lost sanctity, as the boulder may well have been the base of the stone cross which is known to have marked the boundary in Tudor times and which was perhaps destroyed by iconoclasts during the Reformation. The old road probably ran south as far at least as Ainsdale, as during the 13th century – when the route was already over 400 years old – it was used in the annual rushbearing ceremony, when worshippers replaced the church's floor covers with fresh rushes cut from meres like White Otter Mere in Ainsdale. Peter Aughton records the fact that as recently as the 1790s, at the same time that William Sutton was building his South Port Hotel, the rushbearers would pull a traditional North Country rushcart along the Churchgate 'with a string of revellers, accompanied by the morris dance and the performance of ancient fertility rites' before the rushes were strewn on the floor of the church. This ancient ceremony is still celebrated in the church today.

There are odd references to Churchgate in many books about Southport, and the route is carefully delineated in the Churchtown Trail, a leaflet published to inform visitors of the village's history. I found it astonishing that Churchgate was still able to be walked, and was still marked on the town's memory, 1,100 years after first being named. I was also fascinated by the idea of a 'buried' mediaeval road, and intrigued by the unconscious poetry of a string of Victorian 'mediaeval' churches along the Churchgate, crossing invisible parish boundaries with ancient names: St Peter's, St Luke's, the Holy Family, St Cuthbert's. Once all of North Meols was in the parish of St Cuthbert.

Churchgate crossed Birkdale Common and probably ran through old Birkdale village at the junction of Liverpool Road and Shaftesbury Road, but I joined it where Kew Road crosses Eastbourne Road, with the distant spike of St Peter's Church appearing over the rooftops. Churchgate runs through the eastern suburbia of Southport and walking it today is essentially to make a journey across a Victorian and Edwardian landscape; it has been obliterated in places by new streets, and compromises must be made. Perhaps as recently as the 1880s this was still the sandy track it had been for centuries, but this district was built up at the end of the century and the old track was lost. Eastbourne Road has semi-detached houses and runs of small terraces in red brick, with terracotta ornament. There are also neat cottages made of a darker brick, with stone windowsills and slate roofs. This Victorian road is pleasantly wide and has

St Peter's Church, Birkdale.

an elegant sweep to it, curving to join Cemetery Road, but the traffic at all times of the day is very heavy and there are too many cars; they are parked on the kerbs and crammed onto what were gardens, some bricked over, others just with the front wall demolished. When it was photographed by Henry Sampson, Cemetery Road was called Snuttering Lane and had been for centuries. Is there a link here with the Snotterstone, the official boundary between the old Hundreds of West Derby and Leyland? Do they share a common word meaning a boundary? Perhaps Snuttering Lane marked the limit of land that could be cultivated, or ran along what was roughly the boundary between marsh, farmland and the sand dunes.

The landscape opens up on the right-hand side with the large cemetery on Duke Street, and becomes Cemetery Road and Ash Road, names which have suitably funereal echoes of burials and cremations for this road between churches. There are two old churches here which have found new lives. One has been saved from vandalism and demolition by reinvention as a gym. It still has fine stained glass, although some of its windows are boarded up. It also has some pretty carving which seems to be both Moorish and Gothic, alien Victorian styles almost unheard of today. Further along Cemetery Road is the Family Church, a striking building in red brick and terracotta, stone and stained glass. The names of founders and patrons were carved into the foundation stones, so that their names became a part of the church's history. This is an imposing group of fine buildings, with what looks like church, school and offices all with beautiful and ornate carving, Art Nouveau ironwork and Italian echoes in

columns and arches. It is now a bustling religious centre, a church and a school, and seems busy and friendly.

As Ash Street, Churchgate crosses Scarisbrick New Road, always busy and lined with trees and large houses. St Philip's Church is a massive presence, and was described by Nikolaus Pevsner as 'large and competent'. He adds that St Philip's was built in the style of the 13th century, when the sandy trail of Churchgate was used by pilgrims, mourners and travellers. I like this gentle overlapping of histories, Victorian mediaeval churches along a lost mediaeval road. As Ash Street, the old

Iron gates on Cemetery Road.

pilgrim trail crosses Forest Road and climbs to the bridge over the lost railway stations of Ash Street and St Luke's. The sombre church of St Luke dominates the horizon, a confident and solid building built in red brick, but the route map advises modern Churchgate pilgrims to turn off the straight route and walk past the Blue Anchor public house, onto Tithebarn Road.

The road is immediately quieter after the heavy traffic of Ash Street/St Luke's Road; the houses are smaller but the road is more peaceful. There are few reminders of the mediaeval landscape on this journey, but a tithe barn was a store for the tithes, or taxes of produce, that the farm workers paid to the Church or their manor; this is the first inkling of the mediaeval town ahead of us. Peter Aughton hints at 'some evidence' that there was a tithe barn here in the Middle Ages, although Churchtown would have had one and so this road could have led to the tithe barn there. The long straight roads that the Victorians built here have the names of trees – Maple, Lime, Oak, Poplar – and, further along the old Tithebarn Lane, a small number of groves were laid out; Palm, Laurel and Olive are little roads built alongside the embankments that carry bigger roads over the railway lines. These embankments have been heavily planted with fir trees, almost Mediterranean in their solidity and age, a welcome splash of green in this landscape of red brick, tarmac and blue tiles. The small bell tower of St Luke's Church, described by Pevsner as 'severe and disdainful of enrichment', peers over the rooftops towards the old road. There is another church here, as if they are drawn to this ancient pilgrims' trail; this is the Catholic Church of the Holy Family, with red-brick walls and pretty Gothic windows. The road rises to cross Meols Cop station, where it was necessary to make four roads swell up above ground level, above the station, to form a crossroads, and this has been handled by the Victorians with calm assurance: fine retaining walls of hard grey brick, flights of stone steps, and miles of iron railings, each section joined to the next and disguised by an iron manufacturer's plate, now overpainted and unreadable. There is a distant view of the Methodist church spire on Leyland Road, a Southport landmark rising above the trees, another mediaeval stone echo. In the Middle Ages the only buildings taller than the trees in any parish would have been churches.

Churchgate now runs along Bispham Road, a straight, practical road built up in the late 1880s. It is crossed by the far older Wennington Road, which ran in a straight line towards Blowick and eventually Scarisbrick, roughly along modern Foul Lane. This is another of the old roads in the district and was the route from the canal taken by the earliest visitors to the new resort of South Port; from Wennington Road they turned onto the old road of Roe Lane and so eventually joined Lord Street. The handsome buildings on this stretch of Wennington Road are late Victorian, with playful Arts-and-Crafts details, bull's-eye windows, external plasterwork and large bay windows. The buried pilgrim trail of Churchgate here crosses Roe Lane and passes the first old buildings I have seen, the cottages facing Roe Lane across their old kitchen gardens, which are 300–400 years old. Roe Lane is still a busy traffic artery, but beyond is an arrow-straight road called Churchgate, to commemorate the old road. Modern Churchgate is a wealthy road of 1920s semi-detached houses, a road of large cars, smart paving and neat mock-Tudor houses. After the heavy traffic of Roe Lane, it is quiet enough to hear birdsong, but it is very straight and makes for dull walking. At the very end is a modern road called King's Hey Drive; 'hey' suggests a small farm or a croft, and perhaps this is an unconscious echo of the mediaeval farms that once stood here.

Old Churchgate makes a dog-leg at the end of modern Churchgate as the road alignments have been knocked by the demands of 1920s house-building, and then enters Churchgate proper, a narrow lane wide enough for only one car or a wagon at a time. Here at last is a flavour of how the road looked approaching Churchtown 600 or 800 years ago: low cottages, smart gardens and whitewashed walls. Today these cottages have security alarms and seem a little defensive, but they are real cottages, fingertips of the old town pushing out into the surrounding suburbia. There are thatched cottages at last, a slate-roofed terrace, large stone setts in the lane after an hour walking on tarmac, flagstones and concrete. These are the scuffed edges of Churchtown itself, and the low cottages are overlooked by another brick religious building, this time a United Methodist church with stone Gothic details – a solid and red-faced John Bull of a church. From here the pilgrim trail joins Botanic Road and leads to the heart of the old village, and the church of St Cuthbert on the village green.

Churchtown

Churchtown was a thriving village when Southport was sand dunes, and Lord Street a shallow valley prone to flooding. Its white cottages are surrounded by suburbs of Victorian red brick, but it is a wealthy, pretty urban village with antique shops, tea rooms and an upmarket garden centre. Churchtown also has the Botanic Gardens and Museum, and the occasionally open Meols Hall, to attract visitors. The streets in the heart of the village are straight enough but seem arbitrary, as if they have been randomly driven through the collection of cottages; half-timbered thatched houses line the streets, but everywhere there are little cobbled alleyways leading to other cottages behind them, as if it is a mere turn of fate that they are not on the main roads. The old buildings are low and crooked, lumpy with centuries of whitewash, renovations and over-plastering, and all seem to have thatched roofs and black woodwork, perhaps a local tradition. The church is relatively modern, with very little dating from before the 18th century, but the first church was possibly a shelter housing the body of St Cuthbert on his journey across northern England in the early Middle Ages, or a shrine

Slate roofs and red brick – the end of Churchgate as it approaches Churchtown.

The end of the pilgrims' trail – Churchgate as it approaches Botanic Road in Churchtown.

The church of St Cuthbert, Churchtown.

The Bold Arms, Churchtown.

Trap Lane (now Southbank Road) off Churchgate, photographed by Henry Sampson in 1860.

The Hesketh Arms, once run by William Sutton.

commemorating his brief rest here. Some surviving walls of an old building, hastily built of wattle and daub, were found during restoration work in the 1860s.

Churchtown grew up around the church of St Cuthbert, and is centred on the streets and green near the church and Meols Hall; Church and manor are still strong here and the village's two pubs are named after the local gentry, Hesketh and Bold. The Hesketh Arms sits on the pleasantly shaggy village green near the church, and was once run by William Sutton. It was his business acumen that built the South Port Hotel for the new craze of sea bathing, which in turn started the development of South Hawes into South Port. The Botanic Gardens Museum has an imaginative re-creation of a room in the South Port Hotel, a gloomy, creaking place lit by candles. Some of Sutton's possessions have survived: his violin, a heavy chest of drawers and some of the giant beer jugs from the old hotel. One of his account books has also survived and I was able to sit in the pub he used to run and look at photographs of his ledger, to see the South Port Hotel's accounts for 1802 in William Sutton's handwriting. I like this sort of layered history, this crossing of time, and it made the modern Hesketh Arms seem more of an 18th-century inn to me. The pub is sympathetically decorated, open rooms divided by floors

Thatch and whitewash – the old cottages of Churchtown.

Street lamp, the Hesketh Arms.

and colour into dining rooms and inglenooks. There are earthenware jars and old plates and bottles on the walls, which suddenly seemed to have come from one of Sutton's inns. And it occurred to me that Sutton would have recognised many of the noises and the atmosphere – the smells of cooking food and tobacco smoke, laughter, the clatter of plates, the demands of customers.

There is plenty of old Churchtown that Sutton would recognise, plenty of the old, low cottages left, and fingers of Churchtown run out into the surrounding suburbs, odd cottages and farm buildings on the corners of modern roads. But they are isolated now from the village, marooned curiosities in a sea of red-brick houses built as Churchtown and Marshside began to be subsumed by Southport in the late 19th century and became similar to middle-class housing all over the town. Old place names such as Knob Hall Lane and Cotty's Brow still survive in Marshside and many of the cottages are still here; some are still recognisable, some are celebrated, but too many have been buried in pebble-dashing and cottage kitsch, decorated with wagon wheels and bay windows, bad cobbles and false wells so that they disappear into the surrounding urban growth. What few cottages survive have been drowned in a sea of boring suburbia, and there is not much of interest in Marshside today.

Old Marshside was a scattered village of fishermen's cottages, spreading from the old church towards the salt marsh and vulnerable to sea flooding as a result of the restless anger of the tides. The land has been banked up, flooded, rebuilt and flooded again for many centuries. The local word for a sea defence is cop, and there are many cops all over Southport. It is possible that Churchgate ran northwards from Churchtown along Bankfield Lane, which was originally an embankment built in the 13th century as a defence against the sea. These sea defences have given the town one of its wry stories. A cop called Sugar Houses or Sugar Hillocks stood on the corner of modern Cambridge Road. According to local legend, on a stormy night in the mid-16th century a ship was run aground and deposited its cargo of sugar, which gave the embankment its name. The story goes that the ship was also carrying a new and unusual cargo of vegetables, which the locals planted. This is one of Southport's best stories, that the long-lost fields around Cambridge Road were the first places in England to grow potatoes.

CHAPTER SEVEN

LAND, SEA AND SKY

Time and again on walks across Southport I was reminded of other places. When the weather was bright and warm, the sunlight seemed to seek out the Classical buildings and the town looked Roman to me, a seaside resort built by the Victorians in admiration of the ancients. These were days for random journeys and photography, as the sunlight found the back streets and the small places, the odd walls, the overlooked carving. On days of low cloud and drifting smoky rain Southport felt like a small northern European town, somewhere quiet and out-of-season, like Bruges or Utrecht. The floor tiles, the bricks and the slate roofs gleamed in the grey weather, drawing my eye to Dutch-gabled shop fronts, long straight roads like canals of tarmac, a low skyline dominated by church steeples. Days like these I want to spend in a pub with big wooden tables, sipping a Guinness and watching the crowds. In all weathers the encircling landscapes of market gardens, flat sandy beaches and a wide estuary seem to have more in common with the Netherlands or Belgium than England. Writing about Southport's landscapes I was tempted to define this varied and beautiful area simply by land, sea and sky; but I found it difficult to fit the richness and diversity of the town itself into this plan, and so I wrote about the urban environment separately and explored the rural surroundings as four distinct geographical landscapes. East of the town are the fields and farms of the old mosses and meres, a landscape big enough to deserve a chapter to itself. To the north the farms and glass houses meet the sea defences at Banks and Hesketh Bank. South of the town are the great sand hills of Birkdale and Ainsdale, a landscape of golf courses and nature reserves. And westwards, in the sea out beyond the beach, is a restless shifting expanse of low sandy hills, inches high but dangerous enough to be named and marked on sailors' charts.

As you travel north out of Southport, Marine Drive sweeps in a great bend following the coastline. On the left is the beach, a huge flat empty space which looks as though it runs on forever until it meets the sky. Its size is intimidating, and the large trucks of the sand-winning plant are dwarfed to the size of toys as they grind across the sand towards Horse Bank. The Churchtown road turns off abruptly before the plant and runs across the marshes, open water and low islands of the nature reserve, a chance to see in miniature how the old fens might have looked. The low buildings of Marshside rise reluctantly above the grassy embankment, aware that the salt water has flooded these flat lands many times. The view back into Southport from here has always reminded me of the Dutch paintings of Vermeer or Pieter de Hooch, with round towers and steep roofs rising above the marshland into a grey sky.

Between Marine Drive and the distant estuary is an expanse of salt-grasses and wiry turf, cut with deep salt-water channels and divided by low fences. These fields are still flooded by the tide, which leaves ominous weeds hanging on the wires. This is part of the huge Ribble Estuary Nature Reserve, one of a chain of wetland sites in western Europe which are vital to wildlife; these marshes support over a quarter of a million waders and wildfowl each winter. The white houses and towers of Lytham and the Fylde coast are visible over the estuary, and the rollercoaster coils and Tower at Blackpool

Commercial greenhouses and the spire of St Stephen's Church at Banks.

The sea bank at Crossens.

Banks Reclaimed Marsh.

Above and below: A vast, bleak landscape; waterlogged marshes and drainage ditches beyond the sea defences at Banks.

shimmer across the sandy water, a reminder of another watery landscape. Southport and Blackpool have always seemed to have a Venetian quality to them, these towns surrounded and perhaps defined by water. From here Blackpool's Tower and buildings float above the muddy waters of the Ribble's tidal lagoon, but Southport seems more precariously and defiantly built, on a narrow strip of solid ground between old marshland and shallow sea.

The old Martin Mere and the smaller mosses are drained into the estuary at Crossens by the modern pumping station that controls three great artificial waterways. This modern building, with its glacial stone, is on the romantic Ralph's Wife's Lane, supposedly named for a sailor's wife who pined away here waiting for her husband to return from the sea. The wind can be cold off the estuary, and the modern houses in suburban Crossens seem crouched behind a series of channels and raised banks. Away from the road the embankments are solid and grassy, like old military defences, studded with thorn bushes bent and stunted by the wind, the grass dotted with flowers like yellow stars. The few people in this landscape can be seen for miles, giving them a peculiar vulnerability: an old man on a bicycle, a girl training a horse.

North of Crossens towards Banks the landscape seems to drain of human habitation and colour. The houses stop abruptly and the land dissolves into bands of green

Mud and weeds and wire; the salty marshes beyond the sea bank at Banks.

embankment, brown field-earth, grey sky. Huge fields are planted with vegetables, or given over to glasshouses for more tender crops. This is the beginning of the Lancashire market gardens that sweep around Southport and stretch all the way to Ormskirk, built on the rich agricultural land reclaimed from Martin Mere. It is locally famous for the huge Banks car boot sales on Ralph's Wife's Lane, and I once met a man here selling books and old chairs whose grandfather had been one of the lifeboatmen at Formby Point. He remembered helping his father catch shrimps off the Southport coast – catching them in the morning, boiling them on the range in the kitchen, and selling them or preparing them for market in the afternoon. There are more layers of history here; many of the old shrimper's customers were from eastern Europe, young men and women from Poland and Hungary working as farm labourers in Banks or Hesketh Bank. I often wonder what they make of this landscape. Does it seem English to them, this bleak flat place of low fields, sea defences, never-ending winds? Away from the busy main road towards Preston, the lanes are long and straight or curve along drainage ditches and boundaries a few feet above the level of the fields, narrow causeways crossing the land. Towards the sea is a silent flat landscape of few trees, wide fields and high hedges, protected by the sea embankments. Without this I imagine the sea and the sand would create a vast hinterland of salt marsh and tidal mudflats, dotted with low-lying grassy islands, flooded in winter or at seasonal high tides and only stopped perhaps by sand dunes or higher banks inland. St Cuthbert's at Churchtown used to stand on an island above the salt marshes, and Crossens' name remembers a headland with a cross on it, perhaps a landmark for travellers marking the northern Churchgate route to St Cuthbert's itself.

On the Banks Enclosed Marsh the marshes have been tamed. Large rectangular fields of vegetables have been reclaimed from the salt and the tides, defined by deep ditches which cross the landscape in ordered lines. Here too the tall embankment has ancient thorn trees growing on it, presumably to aid stability, but here they have become bent and gnarled by the salt wind. Neatly square or rectangular woods such as Cross Bank Covert have been planted for windbreaks and as cover for the birds. There is shooting on the salt marshes between September and February, but this desolate shoreline is a haven for wild birds – oystercatchers, shelduck, lapwings, the clatter of pheasants rising from the ditches. The approach of winter in Southport is marked by the great skeins of geese which fly over from late September, and when their weird haunting cries are heard over the town they are flying between these rich marshes and the safe waters of the bird sanctuary at Martin Mere. In summer the marshes are grazed by cattle, which in turn enriches the soil and improves it for the wintering birds. Perhaps the architect of the small church of St Stephen in the Banks absorbed this patient Dutch atmosphere, as the spire rising over the village seems to resemble the onion-bellied church spires of Holland and Germany, a further echo for me of northern Europe.

From the great embankment near Banks the salt marshes and mud flats of the Ribble estuary stretch away into the distance, with the buildings of the Fylde coast on the horizon and the Lake District fells beyond. The land is flat, and the skies here seem immense, the expanse of fields behind broken only by a line of farm buildings or a straggling hamlet. The embankment must protect it well, as Banks doesn't seem as hunched against the wind as Crossens. It is strung out along the straight roads, a quiet place with very little traffic, quiet enough to explore freely on foot. There are some sturdy but pretty Victorian cottages and barns in the heart of the village. The graveyard around the church is full of everyday tragedy and local names; Bond, Peet, Blundell, Howard and Abram. The Abram family lost men in both world wars, and a William Abram was drowned in Crossens Pool in an accident in September 1901, which claimed two other lives. Banks is a 19th-century village with modern commuter estates, but here there is the mood of an older country, of families linked by marriage and attached to the soil and the waters for centuries.

This area has always had an ambivalent relationship with the sea. The fields were partially reclaimed from the water and the sand is not very far from the surface, which perhaps accounts for the chalky white colour of the soil. This is a defensive landscape, dug in against the threat of the sea: a landscape of embankments, escarpments, trenches. This is reflected in the local names – Banks, High Brow, Bank View Farm, Marsh Road, Far Banks. The very name Banks suggests both sand hills in the sea and defensive walls. North-east of the village the road shadows the sea defences above fields and ditches towards Hundred End, which was the limit of the mediaeval administrative district centred on West Derby. This Liverpool suburb once had a castle which dominated Lancashire, from Garston on the Mersey to Hundred End here on the estuary of the Ribble. I have spent most of my life in this mediaeval administrative district, and it feels strange to stand on its invisible border, a boundary now devoid of meaning. Nothing tells me today that I am leaving the Hundred of West Derby and entering the Hundred of Leyland, but once the boundary was marked by the Snotterstone. This word surely has a link with Snuttering Lane in old Birkdale, which seems to me to have marked a fine line between marsh and sand dune, another kind of boundary. The Snotterstone was a large glacial boulder 'keeping its lonely vigil on the mudflats for centuries, and sometimes serving as a landmark for travellers along the coast,' in Peter Aughton's poetic phrase. I imagine that the men drawing up the boundaries between the hundreds used many such existing landmarks. Snotterstone defined the boundary for hundreds of years, but as districts changed it was no longer used, and slowly sank into the ground. Perhaps it sank beyond sight, and could no longer be used to define boundaries. It was rediscovered by the local antiquarian Reverend Bulpit in about 1900, who set teams of men to finding it, but he seems not to have photographed it. Today it has disappeared once again.

On the Hesketh shoreline, a watercourse called the Hundred End Gutter once carried water into the Ribble's wide, shallow estuary, which was formed by the river carrying mud and soil down from the Lancashire hills. The sediment is added to sandbanks, forming an enormous area of shifting sands and silting channels, a place far bigger than the fields, far bigger even than Southport. In contrast to the man-made fields and embankments, this watery landscape was formed naturally, by tide, storm and wind, and by the tiny movements of billions of grains of sand. To the layman it is difficult to tell one bank from another, or even where one ends and another begins, but from further south at Southport pier it is easy to see the small rivers that glint in the sunshine, carving shallow channels through the clay and gravel and defining new sandbanks. These unreliable waters and sands are the reason that the coastal pleasure steamers stopped visiting Southport pier in 1923; the watery hills are a danger to shipping as they move constantly, silting channels and changing shape, taking decades to move across the estuary like clouds. They have wrecked many vessels sailing from Preston or Liverpool. The tragedy of the *Mexico* is the most famous, but there are countless stories of wrecks along this coast and until recently the wreck of the *Chrysopolis* could be seen from the pier, rusting metal engine casing encrusted with barnacles.

The land and the sea and the sky meet in this strange landscape. Where does it begin? Where does it end? The sands of Blackpool and Lytham join the estuary, there are banks here at Hundred End and enormous low hills in between. The sky is reflected in the brown water, which sometimes seems more sand than water. The grains are dropped by the exhausted river, or drift, suspended; this coastline is notorious for quicksand. With the daily changes in weather and tide the banks of sand are at one time dry and hard, then waterlogged and treacherously soft, saturated with water and air. Charting this coastline is a desperate race to map the sand banks before they move, grow, disappear; every chart of this estuary is different. The names rise into usage and fall from memory as the landscape changes and moves; they are as shifting as the places they define, and have a strange, blunt poetry. Water-valleys are called channels, pools, gutters, and holes; the low hills are called banks, brows, hills, breasts, wharves. The silts have given the name to the Marl Hole, a deeper sea-pool which once pierced the Wharf, a giant bank north-west of Crossens, but 'marl' also has a nautical meaning, so perhaps the pool was used for repairs to ships. On older charts there was a bank called the Seldom Seen, which must have been particularly low-lying. There was once a Butter Wharf, a low spit of sand which was later swallowed by the biggest of the banks. Why Butter? Names and meanings shift like the sands; there was once a channel called Packet Heading, and there is still a small one called Stone Gutter. The violence of these waters is never forgotten and there is a Mad Wharf, a Foulnaze, an Angry Brow. Channels shift and fade – one simply called Gut was renamed Old Gut and New Gut Channel as it moved and silted, eventually becoming South Gut as part of an attempt to direct the Ribble straight out to sea.

The shape-shifting nature of these sand banks was not entirely due to the forces of the water. The constant dredging of the Mersey and attempts to direct the Ribble through the fearsome-sounding 'Ribble Training Walls' has also had an impact on the sands. The banks seem to be swelling into one monster sandbank speared with channels and tiny tributaries, with a channel for the Ribble through the middle. On the most recent Admiralty chart only Great Brow, Horse Bank, Angry Brow, Penfold Channel and Foulnaze seem to have survived from earlier maps. Salters Bank and Crusader Bank have survived near Blackpool to the north, but the gigantic Horse Bank in particular seems to have drowned smaller channels in sand, absorbed lesser banks and spread across the estuary. The many small banks nearer the shore have become Marshside Sands, Banks's Sands and Hesketh Sands, as if the beaches too are growing. In 1909 the channels were described as 'extraordinarily unstable'. In its advice to mariners, the modern chart says: 'Depths in the charted channel are not maintained. The south retaining wall is reported to be broken; the buoys and beacons are unreliable.' This reads more like a war report than a coastal survey, and also suggests a place where

A young woman in the sand dunes in the 1920s, which should surely have been used for advertising this coastline.

human control is weakening. The gigantic sandbanks seem as slowly volatile and capricious as ever, and in a century or a decade will have assumed shapes we cannot imagine.

Sadly the Horse Bank was never used for the exercise of horses, but is rather a corruption of 'hawes', the old Norse word for a sand-dune. Southport was once an empty district called South Hawes, and for millennia the coastline was defined by a line of hills, giant slowly shifting waves of sand which were slowly built up by the wind, torn apart by storms and weathers, and then built up again. In the early 19th century there were sand fields and dunes from the Ribble estuary to the beach resort of Liverpool, where there were fresh and salt-water baths and a landscape of small beaches. Inland they were stabilised by grasses and scrub and eventually trees, as new hills were started on the coast and the land slowly pushed out to sea. In Southport itself the dunes have been dug out and carted away, but still the sand is everywhere. It blows in from the beach to settle in tiny sculpted drifts along Marine Drive, turns garden soil a dusty grey and is excavated in dirty golden mounds during roadworks. It is possible that Southport is built on a long-buried river bed of the Ribble, which could explain the slowly shifting layers of peat, gravel and unexpected depths of sand beneath the town. Even the radio station is called Dune FM.

The inland dunes have been flattened at Birkdale as well, but the sandy hills once ran for many miles away from the sea, possibly as far as the beginning of the marshy ground at Birkdale Moss. At modern Bedford Park there were tall sand dunes, and one in particular was tall enough to be given a flagpole and named the Isle of Wight. This stood next to an old inn called the Ash Tree Inn, near the site of the Portland Hotel, where Southport visitors could eat and drink after visiting the Isle of Wight. Bedford Park itself was once the home of Birkdale Golf Club, whose first course was laid out among the sand dunes here; when they moved out it was planned to leave the large dunes as hills in the new park, but they seem to have been unstable hills, naked of grasses, and the archives have many photographs of houses on Kew Road being almost engulfed by sand. Perhaps the biggest difference between the old Birkdale of cottages and small farms and the new suburban Birkdale is the absence of the great sand hills.

On the dunes overlooking Birkdale Sands the winds rush in from the sea, clear from the Isle of Man or even from Ireland, sighing as they hit the sharp grasses. The evening skies here are vast, pale white blue and drifted with wisps of high cloud. It is a quiet place, an empty place, these low hills near the sea, even though the commuter traffic on the coast road is not far behind me. The dunes are a series of low hills, 20 or 30 feet tall, a wall of sand protecting modern Birkdale from the wind. The dunes have a long narrow strip of salt-grasses in front of them, full of wildflowers and shore larks in summer, wet and boggy in the winter. Behind the first sand-wall are the 'slacks', long

Winter sunset over Birkdale Sands.

Abandoned rope ball, Birkdale Sands.

valleys between the dunes which flood in winter and provide homes for Natterjack toads, many types of hardy wild flowers, thorny bushes with orange-grey berries, marram grass and countless rabbits. One of these slacks was known as the Velvet Walk and was a Southport attraction before the development of Birkdale in the 1850s, a place of emerald turf studded with wildflowers. The modern Velvet Trail through the sand hills is still good for walking as the hills rise and fall, new valleys open up, small rabbit-trails lead to the tops of dunes, where the wind sighs and shifts the sand through the sharp grass, and the evening sky shows me Blackpool or the distant smoky pine trees of Ainsdale. When my father first moved to Sefton from Liverpool 20 years ago, it was the sheer size of the skies that impressed him the most, the sense of the flat land and great dome of sky. It is a place for contemplation and the appreciation of small things: tiny purple flowers, spiny shrubs, the tracks of rabbits being blown away by the wind. It is a painters' landscape, a place of subtle colour, changing perspectives, shifting clouds and sands, but also a place full of history, full of stories. The settlement of Argar Meols stood near here before being destroyed by the sea; somewhere on these hard sands the bodies of the *Mexico* lifeboatmen were washed ashore. And somewhere near here the wreck of the ship itself was beached, to be unloaded and refitted. The beach is quiet and calm today but there are huge pieces of rotted wood, left to stabilise the sand but perhaps originally washed ashore, salt-bleached and redolent of the violence of the sea. These tree trunks and stumps look like the bones of dinosaurs, or ancient aero engines crashed and burned, cooled and drifted with sand.

Perhaps it is not surprising that fliers took advantage of these wide flat sands. The air company Avro ran flights to Blackpool from sands near the Palace Hotel, and the Birkdale Palace Aerodrome was only the third airfield in the country to receive a licence. It is not difficult to imagine the small aeroplanes turning on the hard sands, the excited holidaymakers crouching and running back towards the dunes, the smell of burned fuel, the roar of the engines. John Mulliner's recent book *Sun, Sand and Silver Wings* details the town's involvement in aviation history from before World War One to the air shows and beach displays of the present day, but it is the earliest flights which intrigue me. The first aeroplane landed on the sands at Southport in 1910 and huge crowds turned out to watch the early fliers like Claude Grahame-White and Compton Paterson. The box-kite aeroplanes seem both cumbersome and vulnerable, with spindly frames and bicycle wheels; they look fragile and even home-made. The old photographs are smudged and awkward, capturing the nervousness and excitement of the occasion, the crowds gasping at the novelty of a person controlling a flying machine, of piloting it through the air. The landscape seems to emphasise the fragility of these early aeroplanes, sitting lightly on the sand or dwarfed by the vastness of the sky.

Claude Grahame–White flying at Southport in 1910.

John Mulliner says that the old airfield on Birkdale Sands is still visible, and it was perhaps this long straight stretch of hard sand that attracted the land speed record here. In 1926 Major Henry Seagrave drove at nearly 153mph on the beach between Birkdale and Southport. Perhaps these stories are well known, but I came across them by accident; looking for Southport stories on the Internet I found the Thrust SSC website and an article by Fred Harris. Seagrave's attempt was not the town's only involvement with high-speed cars and the land speed record. For many years the Sunbeam car *Silver Bullet* was owned by a local man, Jack Field, who housed the giant car in the garages of the Palace Hotel. Mr Field didn't break the land speed record in *Silver Bullet*, but in 1934 he reached speeds of over 170mph on Southport Sands. And in 1936 Malcolm Campbell's old car *Bluebird* was run at Southport by its owner, the band leader Billy Cotton, who was then in residence at the Palais de Danse in the town centre. In September of that year he ran *Bluebird* at 121mph on the sand here. Can these stories be true? The story of these gentleman amateurs and their huge cars is astonishing; it probably deserves a book to itself. It is certainly difficult to imagine such an exciting event happening on these quiet sands today.

It surprised me that aeroplanes and racing cars used these sands, as the beach itself is by no means uniformly flat. There are low islands of bone-white shells no more than six inches high, and lagoons of thick oily clay beneath a blanket of wet sand. At sea level, beach level, the tide marks are trails of dead seaweed, branches, plastic bottles, all writing obliterated and covered with tar after weeks at sea. This is a desert place, the sand crossed by Land Rover tracks, ridges and troughs, prehistoric and made this morning by the retreating tide. The beach is so vast that Southport and Birkdale are reduced to a smudge of houses and towers above the sand, and the walk to the sea seems endless, as if no progress is being made. Further out low valleys begin to appear, the arms of the retreating sea, and the ground becomes wetter, paradoxically harder then softer, and there are delicate lines of tide marks, small shells, the smallest particles of sand and wood dropped by the waves. The Land Rover tracks are gently obliterated by the tide and the wind. There are drunken iron posts driven deep into the sand, perhaps markers from the old airstrip; sometimes they are decorated with the number plates of lost cars, burned out or drowned in sand, a strangely Viking celebration of loss. With its history and stories I find it a melancholy place, this huge beach. Flocks of shore birds wheel and sweep through the sky a few feet above the sand, to settle and feed and rise again. Past the pier, I can see Blackpool and the fells behind Barrow, and southwards I can see the pine woods at Ainsdale and Formby Point, and the distant blur that is the Wirral and the Welsh hills. The hard light makes the sea shimmer, and distances become deceptive. Everything seems a long way away. I could walk here forever, but at some point the tide will come in; another lagoon blocks my way to the sea, and I turn for the long walk back to the sand dunes.

INDEX

Craft and Design in Metal

David M Willacy

Head of Art and Design Studies St Albans School
Reviser in CDT GCSE
Examiner in Design (Advanced Level)

Hutchinson
LONDON · SYDNEY · AUCKLAND · JOHANNESBURG

To my wife, Joan

Hutchinson Education

An imprint of Century Hutchinson Limited
Brookmount House, 62–65 Chandos Place, Covent Garden,
London WC2N 4NW

Century Hutchinson Australia Pty Ltd
89–91 Albion Street, Surry Hills,
New South Wales 2010, Australia

Century Hutchinson New Zealand Ltd
PO Box 40-086, Glenfield, Auckland 10, New Zealand

Century Hutchinson South Africa (Pty) Ltd
PO Box 337, Bergvlei 2012, South Africa

First published 1986
Reprinted with corrections 1987, 1989

Illustrations by Cedric Robson

Designed and set in IBM 10pt Pyramid by Tek-Art,
Croydon, Surrey

Printed and bound in Great Britain by
Richard Clay Ltd, Norwich, Norfolk

British Library Cataloguing in Publication Data

Willacy, David M.
  Craft and design in metal.
  1. Metal-work
  I. Title
  684′.09   TS205

ISBN 0-09-160711-6